AF373432

U. G. Krishnamurti

The Natural State

e-artnow 2021

U. G. Krishnamurti

The Natural State

e-artnow, 2021
Contact: info@e-artnow.org

ISBN 978-80-273-4150-4

Contents

1. 1972-1980: India and Switzerland

Whatever you do in the pursuit of truth or reality takes you away from your own very natural state in which you always are. It's not something you can acquire, attain or accomplish as a result of your effort. All that you do makes it impossible for what already is there to express itself. That is why I call this your natural state. You're always in that state. What prevents what is there from expressing itself in its own way is the search. The search is always in the wrong direction, so all that you consider very profound, all that you consider sacred, is a contamination in that consciousness. You may not [Laughs] like the word contamination but all that you consider sacred, holy and profound is a contamination. There's nothing that you can do, it's not in your hands. This is something which I can't give because you have it. It is ridiculous to ask for a thing which you already have. There isn't anything to get from anybody. You have what I have. I say you are there.

* * * * *

I was brought up in a very religious atmosphere. My grandfather was a very cultured man. He knew Blavatsky [the founder of the Theosophical Society] and Olcott, and then, later on, the second and third generations of Theosophists. They all visited our house. He was a great lawyer, a very rich man, a very cultured man and, very strangely, a very orthodox man. He was a sort of mixed-up kid: orthodoxy, tradition on one side and then the opposite, Theosophy and the whole thing on the other side. He failed to establish a balance. That was the beginning of my problem.

[U.G. was often told that his mother had said, just before she died, that he "was born to a destiny immeasurably high." His grandfather took this very seriously and gave up his law practice to devote himself to U.G.'s upbringing and education. His grandparents and their friends were convinced that he was a yoga bhrashta, one who had come within inches of enlightenment in his past life.]

He had learned men on his payroll and he dedicated himself for some reason "I don't want to go into the whole business" to create a profound atmosphere for me and to educate me in the right way, inspired by the Theosophists and the whole lot. And so, every morning those fellows would come and read the Upanishads, Panchadasi, Nyshkarmya Siddhi, the commentaries, the commentaries on commentaries, the whole lot, from four o'clock to six o'clock, and this little boy of five, six or seven years "I don't know" had to listen to all that crap. So much so that by the time I reached my seventh year I could repeat most of those things, the passages from the Panchadasi, Nyshkarmya Siddhi and this, that and the other.

So many holy men visited my house "the Ramakrishna Order and the others; you name it, and those fellows had somehow visited that house" that was an open house for every holy man. So, one thing I discovered when I was quite young was that they were all hypocrites: they said something, they believed something, and their lives were shallow, nothing. I lived in the midst of people who talked of these things everlastingly "everybody was false, I can tell you. So somehow, what you call existentialist nausea" revulsion against everything sacred and everything holy" crept into my system and threw everything out.

That was the beginning of my search. I did everything, all the austerities. I was so young but I was determined to find out if there was any such thing as enlightenment. I wanted that very much. Otherwise, I wouldn't have given my life. Then my real search began. All my religious background was there in me. Then I started exploring. For some years I studied psychology and also philosophy, Eastern and Western, mysticism, all the modern sciences, everything. The whole area of human knowledge I started exploring on my own.

Before my forty-ninth year I had so many powers, so many experiences, but I didn't pay any attention to them. The moment I saw someone I could see their entire past, present and future without their telling me anything. I didn't use them. I was wondering, puzzled, you see, "Why do I have this power?" Sometimes I said things and they always happened. I couldn't figure out the mechanism of that. I tried to. They always happened. I didn't play with it. Then it had certain unpleasant consequences and created suffering for some people.

* * * * *

[U.G. was travelling all over the world, still lecturing. In 1955, leaving his daughters in India, he and his wife moved to the United States in search of treatment for his son Vasant's polio. By 1961 his money was finished, and he felt beginning within him a tremendous upheaval which he could not and did not wish to control, and which was to last six years and end with the 'calamity'. His marriage broke up. He put his wife and sons "a second, Kumar, had been born in Chicago" on a plane to India, and he went to London. He arrived penniless and began roaming the city. For three years he lived idly in the streets. His friends saw him as heading on a headlong course downhill, but he says that at the time his life seemed perfectly natural to him. Later, religious-minded people were to use the mystics' phrase 'the dark night of the soul' to describe those years, but in his view there was "no heroic struggle with temptation and worldliness, no soul-wrestling with urges, no poetic climaxes, but just a simple withering away of the will."]

All kinds of funny things happened to me. I remember when I rubbed my body like this, there was a sparkle, like a phosphorous glow, on the body. She [Valentine] used to run out of her bedroom to see "she thought there were cars going that way in the middle of the night. Every time I rolled in my bed there was a sparkling of light [Laughs] and it was so funny for me" "What is this?" It was electricity "that is why I say it is an electromagnetic field. At first I thought it was because of my nylon clothes and static electricity; but then I stopped using nylon. I was a very skeptical heretic, to the tips of my toes, I never believed in anything; even if I saw some miracle happen before me, I didn't accept that at all" such was the make-up of this man. It never occurred to me that anything of that sort was in the making for me.

Very strange things happened to me, but I never related those things to liberation or freedom or moksha, because by that time the whole thing had gone out of my system. I had arrived at a point where I said to myself "Buddha deluded himself and deluded others. All those teachers and saviors of mankind were damned fools "they fooled themselves" so I'm not interested in this kind of thing anymore," so it went out of my system completely. It went on and on in its own way "peculiar things" but never did I say to myself, "Well, [Laughs] I am getting there, I am nearer to that." There is no nearness to that, there is no farawayness from that, there is no closeness to that. Nobody is nearer to that because he is different, he is prepared. There's no readiness for that; it just hits you like a ton of bricks.

The whole thing is finished for me and that's all. The linking gets broken and once it is broken it is finished. Then it is not once that thought explodes "every time a thought arises it explodes. The division cannot stay there, it's a physical impossibility. You don't have to do a thing about it. That is why I say that when this explosion takes place (I use the word explosion because it's like a nuclear explosion) it leaves behind chain-reactions. Every cell in your body has to undergo this change.

It's an irreversible change. There's no question of your going back. It is like a nuclear explosion. It shatters the whole body. It is not an easy thing. It is the end of the man, such a shattering thing that it blasts every cell, every nerve in your body. I went through terrible physical torture at that moment; not that you experience the explosion" you can't experience the explosion "but its after-effects. The fallout is the thing that changes the whole chemistry of your body. The senses are operating now without any coordinator or center, that's all I can say. Unless that alchemy or change in the whole chemistry takes place, there is no way of freeing this organism from thought, from the continuity of thought.

The blinking of the eyes stopped and then there were changes in taste, smell and hearing. I noticed that my skin was soft like silk and had a peculiar kind of glow, a golden color.

I no longer spend time in reverie, worry, conceptualization and the other kinds of thinking that most people do when they're alone. My mind is only engaged when it's needed, for instance when you ask questions, or when I have to fix the tape-recorder or something like that. My memory is in the background and only comes into play when it's needed, automatically. When it's not needed there is no mind here, there is no thought; there is only life.

My body had gone away and it has never come back. The points of contact are all that is there for the body. Nothing else is there for me because the seeing is altogether independent of the sense of touch here. I had discovered that all my senses were without any coordination. I felt the life energy drawing to a focal point from different parts of my body. Even now it happens to me. The hands and feet become cold, the body becomes stiff, the heartbeat slows down, the breathing slows down and then there is a gasping for breath. Up to a point you are there. You breathe your last breath, as it were, and then you are finished.

What happens after that, nobody knows. How long it lasted I don't know. I can't say anything about that because the experiencer was finished. There was nobody to experience that death at all. So that was the end of it. I got up. The things that had astonished me that week had become permanent fixtures. I call all these events a calamity because from the point of view of one who thinks this is something fantastic, blissful, full of love, ecstasy and all that kind of a thing, this is physical torture. Not a calamity to me but to those who have an image that something marvelous is going to happen.

It's something like you imagine New York. You dream about it. You want to be there. When you are actually there, nothing of it is there. It is a godforsaken place and even the devils have probably forsaken that place. It's not the thing that you had sought after and wanted so much but totally different.

What is there you really don't know. You have no way of knowing anything about that. There is no image here. Then suddenly, there was an outburst of tremendous energy shaking the whole body, vibrating. It lasted for hours. I couldn't bear it but there was nothing I could do to stop it. There was a total helplessness. This went on and on, day after day. Whenever I sat, it started" this vibration like an epileptic fit or something. Not even an epileptic fit; it went on for days. It was a very painful process because the body has limitations. It has a form, a shape of its own.

So when there is an outburst of energy which is not your energy or my energy but God's (call it by any name you like) it is like a river in spate. The energy that is operating there does not feel the limitations of the body. It is not interested. It has its own momentum. It is a very painful thing. It is not ecstatic, blissful and all that rubbish, stuff and nonsense. It is really a painful thing.

Oh I suffered for months before and after that, everybody has "a great cascade; not one but thousands. It went on and on for months. It's a very painful experience, painful in the sense that the energy has a peculiar operation of its own. It is clockwise, counterclockwise, and then it is this way, and then this way, and then this way. Like an atom, it moves inside" not in one part of your body "the whole body. It is as if a wet towel were being wrung to get rid of the water. It is like that" the whole of our body. It's such a painful thing. It goes on even now. You can't invite it. You can't ask it to come. You can't do anything. It gives you the feeling that it is enveloping you, that it is descending on you.

Every time it is new. Very strange, every time it comes in a different way. So you don't know what is happening. You lie down on your bed and suddenly it begins. It begins to move slowly like ants. I'd think there were bugs in my bed, jump out, look, see no bugs, then I'd go back, then again. The hairs are electrified. So it slowly moves. There were pains all over the body. Thought has controlled this body to such an extent that when that loosens, the whole metabolism is agog. The whole thing was changing in its own way without my doing anything. Every cell started changing and it went on and on for six months. In all, it took three years for this body to fall into a new rhythm of its own. I behaved normally, I didn't know what was happening. It was a strange situation.

The state is something natural. Do you see the swellings here? Yesterday was the new moon. The body is affected by everything that is happening around you. It is not separate. Whatever is happening there is also happening here. There is only the physical response. This is affection.

Your body is affected by everything that is happening around you, and you can't prevent this for the simple reason that the armor that you have built around yourself is destroyed. So it is very vulnerable to everything that is happening there.

There are certain glands. These ductless glands are located in exactly the same spots where the Hindus speculated the chakras are. They have feelings, extraordinary feelings. There is one gland here which is called the thymus gland. Doctors tell us that is active through childhood until puberty then becomes dormant. In your natural state that gland is reactivated.

[Up and down his torso, neck and head, his friends observed swellings of various shapes and colors which came and went at intervals. On his lower abdomen, the swellings were horizontal, cigar-shaped bands. Above the navel was a hard, almond-shaped swelling. A hard, blue swelling like a large medallion in the middle of his chest was surmounted by another smaller, brownish-red, medallion-shaped swelling at the base of his throat. These were as though suspended from a varicolored, swollen ring "blue, brownish and light yellow" around his neck. His throat was swollen to a shape that made his chin seem to rest on the head of a cobra, as in the traditional images of Shiva. Just above the bridge of the nose was a white, lotus-shaped swelling. All over the head the small blood vessels expanded, forming patterns like the stylized lumps on the heads of Buddha statues. The arteries in his neck expanded and rose, blue and snake-like, into his head.]

* * * * *

If somebody hurts himself there, that hurt is felt here "not as a pain, but there is a feeling, you see" you automatically say "Ah!" This actually happened to me when I was staying in a coffee plantation: a mother started beating a child, a little child, you know. She was mad, hopping mad, and she hit the child so hard, the child almost turned blue. And somebody asked me "Why did you not interfere and stop her?" I was standing there "I was so puzzled, you see. "Who should I take pity on, the mother or the child?" "that was my answer" "Who is responsible?" Both were in a ridiculous situation: the mother could not control her anger, and the child was so helpless and innocent. This went on "it was moving from one to the other" and then I found all those things [marks] on my back. So I was also part of that. (I am not saying this just to claim something.) That is possible because consciousness cannot be divided. Anything that is happening there is affecting you "this is affection, you understand? There is no question of your sitting in judgement on anybody; the situation happens to be that, so you are affected by that. You are affected by everything that is happening there.

Consciousness is, of course, not limited. If he is hurt there, you also are hurt here. If you are hurt, there is an immediate response there. I can't say about the universe, the whole universe, but in your field of consciousness, in the limited field in which you are operating at that particular moment, you are responding" not that you are responding.

And all the other glands also here... There are so many glands here; for example, the pituitary "'third eye', 'ajna [command] chakra', they call it. When once the interference of thought is finished, it is taken over by this gland: it is this gland that gives the instructions or orders to the body; not thought any more; thought cannot interfere. (That is why they call it that, probably. I'm not interpreting or any such thing; perhaps this gives you an idea.) But you have built an armor created an armor with this thought, and you don't allow yourself to be affected by things. But you have built an armor, created an armor, with this thought and you don't allow yourself to be affected by things.

Since there is nobody who uses this thought as a self-protective mechanism it burns itself up. Thought undergoes combustion "ionization, if I may use your scientific term. Thought is, after all, vibration. When this kind of ionization of thought takes place it sometimes covers the whole body with an ash-like substance. Your body is covered with that when there is no need for thought at all. When you don't use it what happens to that thought? It burns itself out" that is the energy "it's a combustion. The body gets heated, you know. There is tremendous heat in the body as a result of this, and so the skin is covered" your face, your feet, everything "with this ash-like substance. That's one of the reasons why I express it in pure and simple physical and physiological terms. It has no psychological content at all. It has no mystical content. It has no religious overtones at all, as I see it. I am bound to say that and I don't care whether you accept it or not. It is of no importance to me.

This kind of a thing must have happened to so many people. It is not something that one is specially prepared for. There are no purificatory methods necessary. There is no spiritual practice necessary for this kind of a thing to happen, no preparation of any kind. The consciousness is so pure that whatever you are doing in the direction of purifying that consciousness is adding impurity to it. Consciousness has to flush itself out, it has to purge itself of every trace of holiness, every trace of unholiness, everything. Even what you consider sacred and holy is a contamination in that consciousness.

It is not through any volition of yours. When once the frontiers are broken "not through any effort of yours, not through any volition of yours" then the floodgates are open and everything goes out. In that process of flushing out you have all these visions. It's not a vision outside there or inside of you. Suddenly, your whole consciousness takes the shape of those people who have come into this state. Not great men, not the leaders of mankind, it is very strange, but only those people to whom this kind of a thing happened.

Hundreds of people, probably something happened to so many hundreds of people. This is part of history "so many rishis, some Westerners, monks, so many women, and sometimes very strange things. You see, all that people have experienced before you is part of your consciousness. They run out of your consciousness because they cannot stay there any more, because all that is impurity, a contamination there.

You can say probably it is because of the impact on the human consciousness of the explosions of all those saints, sages and saviors of mankind that there is this dissatisfaction in you, that whatever is there is all the time trying to burst out, as it were. Maybe that is so. I can't say anything about it. You can say that they are there because they are pushing you to this point and once the purpose is achieved they have finished their job and they go away. But this flushing out of everything good and bad, holy and unholy, sacred and profane, has got to happen. Otherwise, your consciousness is still contaminated, still impure. During that time, it goes on and on, there are hundreds and thousands of them. Then, you see, you are put back into that primeval, primordial state of consciousness.

Once it has become pure, of and by itself, then nothing can touch it, nothing can contaminate that any more. All the past up to that point is there but it cannot influence your actions any more. All these visions and everything were happening for three years after the calamity. Now the whole thing is finished. The divided state of consciousness cannot function at all any more. It is always in the undivided state of consciousness.

Nothing can touch that. Anything can happen. The thought can be a good thought, a bad thought. It doesn't matter what comes there "good, bad, holy, unholy. The whole thing is finished. That is why I have to use the phrase religious experience, not in the sense in which you use the word religion. It puts you back to the Source. You are back in that primeval, primordial, pure state of consciousness. Call it awareness or whatever you like. In that state, things are happening and there is nobody who is interested, nobody who is looking at them. They come and go in their own way.

The most puzzling and bewildering part of the whole thing was when the sensory activities began their independent careers. There was no coordinator linking the senses. Like a baby I had to learn everything all over. All the knowledge was in the background and never came to the forefront, you see. But I knew that something really fantastic had happened inside. What it was I didn't know but that didn't bother me. That bewildering situation continued for a long time. All the knowledge was in the background. It's the same situation even now. When I am looking at something I really don't know what I'm looking at. That is why I say it is a state of not knowing. I really don't know. Once you are there through some luck, some strange chance, from then on everything happens in its own way.

You are always in a natural state. There is no question of going in and out of it, you are always there. It is a state of not knowing, you really don't know what you are looking at. I can't do anything about it, there is no question of my going back or anything, it is all finished. It is operating and functioning in a different way.

Somehow, you see, by some luck, by some strange chance, this kind of thing happens, and the whole thing is finished for you. The background is the only thing that can express itself. What else is there? My expression of it is the background "how I struggled, my path, how I rejected the paths of others. Up to that point I can say what I did or what I did not do and that it did not help me in any way.

If people come and ask me questions I answer. If they don't it makes no difference to me. I have not set myself up in the holy business of liberating people. I have no particular message for mankind except to say that all holy systems for obtaining enlightenment are bunk and that all talk of arriving at a psychological mutation through awareness is poppycock. Psychological mutation is impossible. The natural state can happen only through biological mutation.

* * * * *

There is no teaching of mine and never shall be one. A teaching implies a method or a system, a technique or a new way of thinking to be applied in order to bring about a transformation in your way of life. What I am saying is outside the field of teachability. It is simply a description of the way I am functioning. It is just a description of the natural state of man. This is the way you, stripped of the machinations of thought, are also functioning. The natural state is not the state of a self-realized, God-realized man. It is not a thing to be achieved or attained. It is not a thing to be willed into existence. It is there. It is the living state.

This state is just the functional activity of life. By life I do not mean something abstract but the life of the senses functioning naturally without the interference of thought. Thought is an interloper which thrusts itself into the affairs of the senses. It has a profit motive. Thought directs the activity of the senses to get something out of them and uses them to give continuity to itself.

Your natural state has no relationship whatsoever with the religious states of bliss and ecstasy. They lie within the field of experience. Those who have led man on his search for religiousness throughout the centuries have perhaps experienced those religious states, so can you. They are thought-induced states of being and as they come so do they go. All are trips in the wrong direction. They are all within the field of time. Timeless can never be experienced, grasped, contained, much less given expression to, by any man. That beaten track will lead you nowhere. There is no oasis situated yonder. You are stuck with the mirage.

* * * * *

This state is a physical condition of your being. It is not some kind of psychological mutation. It is not a state of mind into which you can fall one day and out of the next. You can't imagine the extent to which, as you are now, thought pervades and interferes with the functioning of every cell in your body. Coming into your natural state will blast every cell, every gland, every nerve. It is a chemical change. An alchemy of some sort takes place. But this state has nothing to do with the experiences of chemical drugs. Those are experiences, this is not.

* * * * *

Does such a thing as enlightenment exist? To me what does exist is a purely physical process. There is nothing mystical or spiritual about it. If I close the eyes some light penetrates through the eyelids. If I cover the eyelids there is still light inside. There seems to be some kind of a hole in the forehead which doesn't show but through which something penetrates. In India that light is golden, in Europe it is blue.

There is also some kind of light penetration through the back of the head. It's as if there is a hole running through between those spots in front and back of the skull. There is nothing inside but this light. If you cover those points there is complete, total darkness. This light doesn't do anything or help the body to function in any way, it's just there.

This state is a state of not knowing. You really don't know what you are looking at. All there is inside is wonderment. It is a state of wonder because I just do not know what I am looking at. The knowledge about it, all that I have learned, is held in the background unless there is a demand. When required it comes quickly like an arrow, then I am back in the state of not knowing, of wonder.

You can never understand the tremendous peace that is always there within you that is your natural state. Your trying to create a peaceful state of mind is in fact creating disturbance within you. You can only talk of peace, create a state of mind and say to yourself that you are very peaceful, but that is not peace, that is violence. There is no use in practicing peace or reason to cultivate silence. Real silence is explosive. It is not the dead state of mind that spiritual seekers think. That doesn't mean anything at all. This is volcanic in its nature. It's bubbling all the time "the energy, the life" that is its quality.

Life is aware of itself, if we can put it that way. It is conscious of itself. When I talk of feeling I do not mean the same thing that you do. Actually, feeling is a physical response, a thud in the thymus. The thymus, one of the endocrine glands, is located under the breast bone. When you come into your natural state, sensations are felt there. You don't translate them as good or bad. They are just a thud. If there is a movement outside of you in your field of vision, that movement is also felt in the thymus. The whole of your being is that movement, or vibrates with that sound. There is no separation. This does not mean that you identify yourself with it. There is no you there, nor is there any object. What causes that sensation you don't know. You do not even know that it is a sensation.

Affection (this is not my interpretation of the word) means that you are affected by every-thing, not that some emotion flows from you towards something. The natural state is a state of great sensitivity, but this is a physical sensitivity of the senses, not some kind of emotional compassion or tenderness for others. There is compassion only in the sense that there are no others for me and so there is no separation. Actually, there is always a gap between any two sensations. The coordinator bridges that gap, establishes itself as an illusion of continuity. In the natural state, there is no entity coordinating the messages from the different senses, each sense is functioning independently in its own way.

When there is a demand from outside which makes it necessary to coordinate the senses and come up with a response, still there is no coordinator but there is a temporary state of coordination. There is no continuity. When the demand has been met, again there is only the uncoordinated, disconnected, disjointed functioning of the senses. This is always the case. Once the continuity is blown apart, not that it was ever there but the illusory continuity, it's finished once and for all.

All that you know lies within the framework of your experience, which is of thought. This state is not an experience. I am only trying to give you a feel of it, which is, unfortunately, misleading. When there is no coordinator, there is no linking of sensations, there is no trans-lating of sensations. They stay pure and simple sensations. I do not even know that they are sensations. I may look at you as you are talking. The eyes will focus on your mouth because that is what is moving and the ears will receive the sound vibrations. There is nothing inside which links up the two and says that it is you talking.

What functions is a primordial consciousness untouched by thought. The eyes are like a very sensitive camera. The physiologists say that light reflected off objects strikes the retina of the eye and the sensation goes through the optic nerve to the brain. The faculty of sight, of seeing, is simply a physical phenomenon. It makes no difference to the eyes what they are focused on, they produce sensations in exactly the same way. The eyes look on everyone and everything without discrimination. Left to themselves they do not linger but are moving all the time. They are drawn by the things outside. Movement attracts them, or brightness, or a color which stands out from whatever is around it.

There is no self looking. The consciousness is like a mirror reflecting whatever is there outside. The depth, the distance, the color "everything is there, but there is nobody who is translating these things. Unless there is a demand for knowledge about what I am looking at, there is no separation, no distance from what is there. There is a kind of clarity.

The eyes do not blink except when there is sudden danger. This is something very natural because things outside are demanding attention all the time. Then when the eyes are tired they may be open but the vision is blurred. If they stay open all the time, if the reflex action of blinking is not operating, they become dry and there are some glands beyond the outer corners of the eyes, not activated in your case, which act as a watering mechanism. But by practicing not blinking one will not arrive in this state, one will only strain the eyes. Once you are in your natural state, by some luck or some strange chance, all this happens in its own way.

When I am walking and suddenly see something different because the light has changed, this consciousness suddenly expands to the size of the object in front of the body and the lungs take a deep breath. This is pranayama, not hyperventilation or inhaling through one nostril and exhaling through the other. This pranayama is going on all the time. So there is consciousness of a sudden change in the breathing and then it moves on to something else. It is always moving. It does not linger on something which thought has decided is beautiful. There is no one directing.

As for listening, when you leave the sense of hearing alone all that is there is the vibration of the sound. The words repeat themselves inside of you as in an echo chamber. This sense is functioning in just the same way with you except that you think the words you are hearing come from outside of you.

* * * * *

Get this straight "you can never hear one word from anyone no matter how intimately you think you are in relationship with that person. You hear only your own translations always. They are all your words you are hearing. All that the other person's words can possibly be to you is a noise, a vibration picked up by the eardrum and transferred to the nerves which run to the brain. You are translating those vibrations all the time trying to understand because you want to get something out of what you are hearing. When there is no translation, all languages sound the same whether or not your particular knowledge structure speaks a particular language. The only differences are in the spacing of the syllables and in the tune. Languages are melodic in different ways but the appreciation of music, poetry and language is all culturally determined and is the product of thought.

Your movement of thought interferes with the process of touch just as it does with the other senses. Anything you touch is always translated as hard, soft, warm, cold, wet, dry and so on. Without this thought process there is no body consciousness, there are only isolated points of contact, impulses of touch which are not tied together by thought. So the body is not different from the objects around it. It is a set of sensations like any others. Your body does not belong to you.

Perhaps I can give you the feel of this. I sleep for four hours at night no matter what time I go to bed then I lie in bed until morning fully awake. I don't know what is lying there in the bed. I don't know whether I'm lying on my left side or my right side. For hours and hours I lie like this. If there is any noise outside, it just echoes in me. I listen to my heartbeat and don't know what it is.

There are only the sensations of touch from points of contact and the gravitational pull, nothing inside links up these things. Even if the eyes are open and looking at the whole body there are still only the points of contact and they have no connection with what I am looking at. If I want to try to link up these points of contact into the shape of my own body probably I will succeed but by the time it is completed the body is back in the same situation of different points of contact. The linkage cannot stay.

My talking comes out in response to the questions which are asked. I cannot sit and give a talk on the natural state. That is an artificial situation for me. There is nobody who is thinking thoughts and then coming out with answers. This state is expressing itself. I really don't know what I'm saying and what I'm saying is of no importance. You may transcribe my own talking but it will make no sense to me. It is a dead thing.

What is here, this natural state, is a living thing. It cannot be captured by me, let alone by you. It's like a flower. This simile is all I can give. It just blooms. It's there. As long as it is there it has a fragrance which is different and distinct from that of every other flower. You may not recognize it. It's of no importance. You can't preserve its perfume. Whatever you preserve of this is not the living thing. Preserving the expressions, teachings or words of such a man has no meaning. This state has only contemporary value, contemporary expression.

* * * * *

The natural needs of a human being are basic: food, clothing and shelter. You must either work for them or be given them by somebody. If these are your only needs they are not very difficult to fulfill. To deny yourself the basic needs is not a sign of spirituality. But to require more than food, clothing and shelter is a neurotic state of mind.

Is not sex a basic human requirement? Sex is dependent upon thought. In the natural state, there is no build-up of thought. Without that build-up sex is impossible. The body normally is a very peaceful organism and then you subject it to this tremendous tension and release which feels pleasurable to you. Actually, it is painful to the body. But through suppression or attempts at sublimation of sex you will never come into this state.

As long as you think of God you will have thoughts of sex. Ask any religious seeker you may know who practices celibacy whether he doesn't dream of women at night. Why do you weave so many taboos and ideas around this? Why do you destroy the joy of sex? Not that I am advocating indulgence or promiscuity but through abstinence and continence you will never achieve a thing.

There must be a living contact. There are no images here. There is no room for them. The sensory apparatus is completely occupied with the things I am looking at now. And so, if you are totally tuned in to the sensory activity, there is no room for fears about who will feed you tomorrow or for speculation about God, truth and reality. This is not a state of omniscience wherein all of man's eternal questions are answered, rather a state in which the questioning has stopped. It has stopped because those questions have no relation to the way the organism is functioning, and the way the organism is functioning leaves no room for those questions.

The body has an extraordinary mechanism for renewing itself. This is necessary because the senses in the natural state are functioning at the peak of their sensitivity all the time. So when the senses become tired the body goes through death. This is real physical death not some mental state. It can happen one or more times a day. You do not decide to go through this death. It descends upon you.

It feels, at first, as if you have been given an anaesthetic. The senses become increasingly dull, the heartbeat slows, the feet and hands become ice cold and the whole body becomes stiff like a corpse. Energy flows from all over the body towards some point. It happens differently every time. The stream of thoughts continues but there is no reading of the thoughts. At the end of this period you conk out. The stream of thought is cut. There is no way of knowing how long that cut lasts.

There is nothing you can say about that time of being conked out. That can never become part of your conscious existence or conscious thinking. You don't know what brings you back from death. If you had any will at that moment you could decide not to come back. When the conking out is over, the stream of thought picks up exactly where it left off. The dullness ends and clarity returns. The body feels very stiff then slowly it begins to move of its own accord, limbering itself up. It is an extraordinary movement. Those who have observed my body moving say it looks like the motions of a newly born baby. This conking out gives a total renewal of the senses, glands and nervous system. After it, they function at the peak of their sensitivity.

Life is action. Questioning your actions is destroying the expression of life. A person who lets life act in its own way without the protective movement of thought has no self to defend. What is keeping you from being in your natural state? You are constantly moving away from yourself. You want to be happy either permanently or at least for this moment. You are dissatisfied with your everyday experiences and so you want some new ones. You want to perfect yourself, to change yourself. You are reaching out, trying to be something other than what you are. It is this that is taking you away from yourself.

Society has put before you the ideal of a perfect man. No matter in which culture you were born, you have scriptural doctrines and traditions handed down to you to tell you how to behave. You are told that through due practice you can even eventually come into the state attained by the sages and saints, and so you try to control your behavior, to control your thoughts, to be something unnatural. Your effort to control life has created a secondary movement of thought within you which you call the self.

This movement of thought within you is parallel to the movement of life but isolated from it. It can never touch life. You are a living creature yet you lead your entire life within the realm of this isolated, parallel movement of thought. You cut yourself off from life. That is something very unnatural. The natural state is not a thoughtless state. That is one of the greatest hoaxes perpetrated for thousands of years. You will never be without thought. Being able to think is necessary to survive but in this state thought stops choking you. It falls into its natural rhythm.

This is the crux of the whole problem. The one that is looking at what you call the self is the self. It is creating an illusory division of itself into subject and object, and through this division it is continuing. This is the divisive nature that is operating in you, in your consciousness. Continuity of its existence is all that interests it. As long as you want to understand yourself or to change yourself into something spiritual, into something holy, beautiful or marvelous, you will continue. If you do not want to do anything about it, it is not there. It's gone.

Through thinking you cannot understand a thing. You are translating what I am saying in terms of the knowledge you already have just as you translate everything else, because you want to get something out of it. When you stop doing that, what is there is what I am describing. The absence of what you are doing "trying to understand or trying to change yourself" is the state of being that I am describing. Because you are not interested in the everyday things and happenings around you, you have invented the beyond, timelessness, God, truth, reality, enlightenment or whatever, and search for it.

* * * * *

There may not be any ultimate truth. You don't know a thing about it. Whatever you know is what you have been told, what you have heard, and you are projecting that information. What you call something is determined by the learning you have about it, and whatever knowledge you have about it is exactly what you will experience. The knowledge creates the experience and the experience then strengthens the knowledge. What you know can never be ultimate reality.

In the natural state the movement of self is absent. The absence of this movement probably is the beyond but that can never be experienced by you. It is when the you is not there. The moment you translate, the you is there. You look at something and recognize it. Thought interferes with the sensation by translating. You are either thinking about something which is totally unrelated to the way the senses are functioning at the moment or else labeling. That is all that is there. The word separates you from what you are looking at, thereby creating the you. Otherwise, there is no space between the two.

Every time a thought is born, you are born. When the thought is gone, you are gone. But the you does not let the thought go and what gives continuity to this you is the thinking. Actually, there is no permanent entity in you, no totality of all your thoughts and experiences. You think that there is somebody who is thinking your thoughts, somebody who is feeling your feelings. That's the illusion. I can say it is an illusion but it is not an illusion to you.

Your emotions are more complex but it is the same process. There is a sensation in you and you name it. This brings into existence the one who is translating this sensation. Self is nothing but a word. This labeling is only necessary when you must communicate. You think the thoughts of your society, feel the feelings of your society and experience the experiences of your society. There is no new experience. So all that any man has ever thought or felt must go out of your system. And you are the product of all that knowledge. That's all you are.

All that you know about what you call thought is what you have been told. You are all the time trying to do something with it because somebody has told you that you must change this or replace that, hold on to the good thoughts and not the bad thoughts. Thoughts are thoughts; they are neither good nor bad.

As long as you want to do something with whatever is there you are thinking. Wanting and thinking are not two different things. Wanting to understand means there is a movement of thought. You are adding momentum to that movement, giving it continuity. The senses function unnaturally in you because you want to use them to get something. Why should you get anything? Because you want the self to continue you are protecting that continuity. Thought is a protective mechanism. It protects you at the expense of something or somebody else.

* * * * *

If you could be in a state of awareness for a single moment once in your life the continuity would be snapped, the illusion of the experiencing structure, the you, would collapse and everything would fall into the natural rhythm. In this state you do not know what you are looking at. That is awareness. If you recognize what you are looking at you are there again experiencing the old, what you know. What makes one person come into his natural state and not another person, I don't know. Perhaps it's written in the cells. It is acausal. It is not an act of volition on your part. You can't bring it about. There is absolutely nothing you can do.

You can distrust any man who tells you how he got into this state. One thing you can be sure of is that he cannot possibly know himself and cannot possibly communicate it to you. There is a built-in triggering mechanism in the body. If the experiencing structure of thought happens to let go, the other thing will take over in its own way. The functioning of the body will be a totally different functioning without the interference of thought except when it is necessary to communicate with somebody. You have to throw in the towel, be totally helpless. No one can help you and you cannot help yourself.

This state is not in your interest. You are only interested in continuity. You want to continue, probably on a different level, and to function in a different dimension, but you want to continue somehow. You wouldn't touch this with a barge pole. This is going to liquidate what you call you, all of you. This structure is born of time and functions in time but does not come to an end through time.

You can't understand what I am saying. It is an exercise in futility on your part to try to relate the description of how I am functioning to the way you are functioning. This is a thing which I cannot communicate nor is any communication necessary. No dialogue is possible. When the you is not there, when the question is not there, what is, is understanding. You are finished. You'll walk out. You will never listen to anybody describing his state or ask any questions about understanding at all.

What you are looking for does not exist. You would rather tread an enchanted ground with beatific visions of a radical transformation of that non-existent self of yours into a state of being which is conjured up by some bewitching phrases. That takes you away from your natural state. It is a movement away from yourself. To be yourself requires extraordinary intelligence. You are blessed with that intelligence. Nobody need give it to you. Nobody can take it away from you. He who lets that express itself in its own way is a natural man.

* * * * *

You see, the animal becomes a flower. That seems to be the purpose if at all there is any purpose in nature. I don't know. There are so many flowers there. Look at them! Each flower is unique in its own way. Nature's purpose seems to be (I cannot make any definitive statement) to create flowers like that, human flowers like that.

Man becomes man for the first time, and that is possible only when he frees himself from the burden of the heritage we are talking about, the heritage of man as a whole. Then only does he become an individual. For the first time he becomes an individual. That is the individual I am talking about. That individual will certainly have an impact on human consciousness. Like when you throw a stone in a pool it sets in motion circular waves. Maybe that's the only hope that man has.

That's the first time such an individual becomes a man. Otherwise, he is an animal. And he has remained an animal because of heritage, because his heritage has made it possible from the point of view of nature for the unfit to remain, or it would have rejected them a long time ago. It has become possible for the unfit to survive "not the survival of the fittest but of those unfit to survive" and religion is responsible for that.

He's not a perfect man. He's not an ideal man. He cannot be a model for others. He becomes freed from all the animal traits in him. Animals follow. Animals create leaders. And the animal traits are still persisting there in man. That is why he creates a leader and follows.

You become yourself. You see, the shock that your dependence on the entire heritage of mankind has been wrong, that realization dawns on you. It hits you like lightning that your dependence on this culture, be it Oriental or Occidental, has been responsible for this situation in you. That applies to the whole as well because the nation is the extension of the individual and the world is the extension of the different nations.

So you are freed from the burden of the past and become for the first time an individual. There is no relationship between these two flowers at all so there is no point in comparing and contrasting the unique flowers that nature has thrown up from time to time. They in their own ways have had their impact. Each flower has its own fragrance.

If it had not been for the heritage of man which we are so proud of we would have had so many flowers like this. It's not that I am interpreting or understanding nature's ways, the purpose of evolution or any such thing. There may not be any such thing as evolution at all. If it had not been for culture, nature would have thrown up many more flowers. It has become a stumbling block to man's freeing himself in his own way. What is responsible for his difficulty is culture. It is of no use to the society at all but it is there.

If it had not been for culture the world would have produced more flowers, different kinds and varieties of flowers, not only the one rose that you are so proud of. You want to turn everything into one model. What for? Whereas, nature would have thrown up from time to time different flowers unique each in its own way, beautiful each in its own way. That possibility has been destroyed by this culture which has a stranglehold on man, which prevents him from freeing himself from the burden of the entire past.

One ceases to be somebody else and is simply what one is. This shock, this lightning, hitting with the greatest force, shatters everything, blasts every cell and gland in the body. The whole chemistry seems to change. There's nothing to certify that but I'm not interested in satisfying anyone's curiosity because I am not selling this. I am not collecting followers and teaching them how to bring about this change. It's something which you cannot bring about through any volition or effort of yours. It just happens. I say it is acausal. What its purpose is I really don't know but it is something, you see.

The whole chemistry of the body changes so it begins to function in its own natural way. That means everything that is poisoned and contaminated by the culture is thrown out of the system. It is thrown out of your system and then that consciousness or life or whatever you want to call it expresses itself and functions in a very natural way. The whole thing has to be thrown out of your system.

This individual is neither a theist nor an atheist nor an agnostic. He is what he is. The movement that has been created by the heritage of man which is trying to make you into something different from what you are comes to an end and what you are begins to express itself in its own way, unhindered, un-handicapped, unburdened by the past of mankind as a whole. Such a man is of no use to the society. On the contrary, he becomes a threat. He doesn't think that he is chosen, chosen by some power to reform the world. He doesn't think that he is a savior or a free or enlightened man. And the moment followers fit him into the tradition, there arises a need for somebody else to break away from that tradition, that is all.

Whatever I say stands or falls by itself. It doesn't need the support of any authority of any kind. That is why such a man is a threat to the society. He's a threat to the tradition because he's undermining the whole foundation of the heritage. My talking to people is incidental. I mean it. Otherwise, I would get up on a platform. What is the point in getting up on a platform? I am not interested. I have no message to give.

It's not in anybody's hands but you have a hundred per cent certainty because it is not that it is my special privilege or that I'm specially chosen by anything. It's there in you. That's what I mean by saying there's no power outside of man. It is the same power, the same life, that is functioning there in you. Something is trying to express itself and the culture is pushing it down. When once it throws the culture out then it expresses itself in its own way.

That is the fragrance of this flower. Such an individual cannot retire into a cave or hide himself. He has to live in the midst of the world. He has no place to go to. That is the fragrance of this flower. When you stop trying to understand what this flower is and what this perfume is which you have never known, there is another flower, not a copy of that flower. The moment you stop trying to compare this, trying to understand and even imagine what this flower is, what its fragrance is, there is a new flower there which has no relationship whatsoever with all the flowers that we have around us.

When this thing happened to me I realized that all my search was in the wrong direction and that this is not something religious, not something psychological, but a purely physiological functioning of the senses at their peak capacities. You want to know what my state is and make it part of knowledge, i.e. the tradition, but knowledge must come to an end. Your wanting to know only adds momentum to your knowledge. It is not possible to know what this is because knowledge is still there and is gathering momentum. The continuity of knowledge is all you are interested in.

I want to make it very clear that there is no movement. You are not going to move from what you are. You haven't even taken one step. There is no need for you to take any step. This consciousness which is functioning in me, in you, is the same. In me it has no frontiers. In you there are frontiers. You are enclosed in that.

Probably, this unlimited consciousness pushes you, I don't know. Not me, I have nothing to do with it. It is like the water finding its own level, that's all. That is its nature. That is what is happening in you. Life is trying to destroy the enclosing thing, that dead structure of thought and experience which is not of its nature. It's trying to come out, to break open. You don't want that. As soon as you see some cracks there you bring some plaster and fill them in and block it again. It doesn't have to be a person that pushes you. Anything teaches you just the same if only you let it.

* * * * *

You will never know what life is. Nobody can say anything about life. You can give definitions but those definitions have no meaning. You can theorize about life but that is a thing which is not of any value to you. It cannot help you to understand anything. When the question burns itself out what is there is energy. You can't say anything about that energy. It is already manifesting itself, expressing itself in a boundless way. It has no limitations, no boundaries. It is not yours, not mine. It belongs to everybody. You are part of that. You are an expression of that. Just as the flower is an expression of life, you are another expression of life.

You are not different from the animal. You don't want to accept that fact. The only difference is that you think. Thinking is there in the animal also but it has become very complex in the case of man. That's the difference. Don't tell me that animals do not think. They do. But in man it has become a very complex structure and the problem is how to free yourself from this structure and use it only as an instrument to function in this world. It has no other use at all. It has only a contingent value "to communicate something, to function in the world" that's all, not philosophical concepts. That has no meaning at all.

Wanting anything other than the basic needs is self-deception. All this thinking has no meaning at all. Thinking is unnecessary except to communicate with somebody. Everyone is talking to themself. It is wearing you out and all methods that we use are adding more and more to that, unfortunately. All techniques and systems are adding to that. There is nothing you can do to end thinking. You see, you have to come to a point where you say to yourself, I am fed up with this kind of thing. Nobody can push you there.

Thought is there when there is a demand for it. When there is no demand for it you don't know whether it is there or not. But when there is a need for it, when there is a demand for it, it is there to guide you and to help you communicate with someone. What decides that demand is not here it is out there. The situation demands its use. It is not self-initiated.

You have no way at all of finding out for yourself the seat of human consciousness because it is all over and you are not separate from that consciousness. For some reason or the other the culture has limited the possibility of the potential evolving into its completeness and wholeness.

Somewhere along the line possibly thought was necessary but it has become the enemy of man now. It has become the enemy of man because the potential of the evolutionary process is thwarted by the culture's creation of a perfect man, a religious man, a gentleman and so on, that is quite the opposite of what is inherent here. Every human being has a unique personality of his own which is trying to express itself.

The culture has created what is called a normal man. You see, character building is in the interests of the continuity of the society. The character building mechanism has suppressed and thwarted what is there inside. It is in this sense that I use the word personality. There is nobody like you anywhere in this world among the six billion people we have. Physiologically speaking, the individual is an extraordinary piece of creation by the evolutionary process. So I say that every individual is unique. Whatever is there is trying to express itself and blossom into a human being.

The human being has lost all of the animal instincts and he has not developed the human instincts. What these people talk of "psychic powers, clairvoyance" they are all human instincts. And they are necessary because there are two things that the human organism is interested in. One: its survival at any cost. That is one of the most important things. It has a survival mechanism of its own which is quite different from the survival mechanism of the movement of thought. The second thing is to reproduce itself. It has to reproduce. These are the two fundamental characteristics of the human organism, the living organism.

The culture has made it impossible for the personality to express itself in its own way because the culture has different ideas. It has created a neurotic state. It has created this divisive movement of thought. This divisive movement has got to come to an end if whatever is there is to express itself and come into flower. That possibility is part of the human mechanism. It is built-in there.

The problem is that anything you do "any movement in any direction on any level" gives continuity to the structure of thought. The separation between mind and body must come to an end. Actually, there is no separation. I have no objection to the word mind but it is not in one particular location or area. Every cell in your system has a mind of its own and its functioning or working is quite different from that of the other cells.

So the whole chemistry of the body has to change. It has to undergo a sort of alchemy, if I may put it that way. Fortunately, there are certain areas in the human organism which are outside the control of thought. This is what I have discovered for myself. They are the glands, what you call the ductless glands. The day you control them that's the end of man. He will lose everything. He will become just a nut and bolt in the social structure. What little freedom he can have, what little opportunity there is for this personality to express itself, will be lost.

These glands are outside the control of thought. A tremendous amount of money is being spent and a lot of research is going on to find out why they are there, what the function of those glands is "the pituitary gland, the pineal gland, the thymus gland and so forth. Unless they are activated, any chance of human beings flowering into themselves is lost.

* * * * *

I can't say there is any such thing as an evolutionary process but there seems to be. What its nature is, what its purpose is, I do not know, but it seems to be trying to create something. Man remains incomplete unless the whole of this human organism blooms into something, like a flower.

* * * * *

Society is there inside, not outside. Culture is part of human consciousness and everything that any predecessor has experienced is part of that. Not that there is an entity which reincarnates. There is no entity there. So the whole business of reincarnation is absurd as far as I am concerned. That is why in your dreams you dream as if you are flying like a bird. Likewise, the sex fantasies man has, the animal postures, The Kama Sutra of Vatsyayana "all that is part of that consciousness which is transmitted from generation to generation.

The genetic is only part of it. Consciousness is a very powerful factor in experiencing things but it is not possible for anybody to find out the content of the whole thing. It is too vast. The day the endocrine glands are controlled it will change the personality of man. If nature had been allowed to go on in its own way everybody would have become a unique flower. The possibility is there of a change taking place which is not progressive. It has to happen in a very sudden and explosive way to break the whole thing.

This has no social, religious or mystical content. Maybe it affects the whole of human consciousness. It is bound to. There is only one mind, one consciousness. Whatever happens here is bound to affect. You see, there is a constant battle going on here between what is here trying to express itself in its own way and the culture preventing it. But you can't do a thing through volition. It has to happen. That is why I say it is acausal.

It seems to have happened to some people during the course of history. Each one has given expression to that uniqueness in their own way according to their background. It is an expression of that background. Nature, in its own way, throws out from time to time some flower, but this end product of human evolution cannot be used by this evolutionary process as a model to create another one. If it throws out one flower, that is it, you see. You can't preserve it. You can't preserve the perfume of that because if you preserve it, it will stink. The evolutionary process or movement is not interested in using the one that it has perfected as a model for further creation. It has a creation of its own.

The one question that this organism is interested in is, How to throw off the whole thralldom, the whole strangling influence of culture? That question is the only question this organism has, not in words, not as a thought "the whole human organism is that one question. I don't know whether I make myself clear. That is the one question, you see, which is throbbing, pulsating, in every cell, in the very marrow of your bones, trying to free itself from this stranglehold. That is the one question, the one thought. That is the savior.

For that question there is no way of finding an answer. With that question it is impossible for one to do anything. So it explodes. When there is no way to move with it, no space, the explosion takes place. That is like a nuclear explosion. It breaks the continuity of thought. Actually, there is no continuity of thought because thoughts are disconnected, disjointed things. But something is linking them up "what you call the self or the center, which is illusory. I can say it is illusory because it is only the knowledge you have about that which creates the identity. All the talk of self-knowledge or self-knowing has no meaning to me. It is within the framework of knowledge. It is playing tricks with itself.

So this continuity comes to an end and thought falls into its natural rhythm. Then it can't link up. The linking gets broken and once it is broken it is finished. Then it is not once that thought explodes "every time that a thought arises it explodes. It is like a nuclear explosion, you see, and it shatters the whole body. It is not an easy thing. It is the end of the man, such a shattering thing that it will blast every cell, every nerve in your body. I went through terrible physical torture at that moment. Not that you experience the explosion "you can't experience the explosion" but its after-effect, the fallout, changes the whole chemistry of your body. Then thought cannot link up any more. The constant demand for experiencing things comes to an end.

This is purely and simply a machine functioning automatically. The mechanism is functioning in an automatic way but with an extraordinary intelligence that is there. It knows what is good for it. There is an tremendous intelligence which is guiding the mechanism of the human body and its interest is protection, to protect its survival. Then the senses become very important factors. They begin to function at their peak capacity without the interference of thought except when there is a demand for it.

Thought is not self-initiated. It always comes into operation on demand. It depends upon the demands of the situation. There is a situation where thought is necessary and so it is there. Thought is only for the purposes of communication. Otherwise, it has no value at all. Then you are guided by your senses and not by your thoughts any more. All this talk of controlling the senses is tommyrot, absolute rubbish. The senses have a built-in mechanism of control. It is not something to be acquired. You can try to control, say, the sense of taste, but in this state you don't have to discipline or control yourself. This physical or human organism or whatever you want to call it is guided by sensory activity alone and not by thinking, not by mind at all.

* * * * *

I tell you, you are not an ordinary being; you are an extraordinary being (Laughter.) There is no one like you. You are 'the one without a second' that the Upanishads talked about. The ideal of the perfection that has been placed before us has put the whole thing on the wrong track. The perfect being doesn't exist at all.

* * * * *

Questioning my actions before and after is over for me. The moral questions about words or actions are no longer there. I have no regrets, no apologies. Whatever I am doing is automatic. In a given situation I am not capable of acting in any other way. I don't have to rationalize, think logically, nothing. That is the one and only action in that particular situation. Next time the action will be different. There are new factors.

You may see it as inconsistency or contradiction. I cannot act in any other way. There's no connection between the two actions. It is physical, not psychological. I don't remember anything that is not happening at that particular moment. There is no reaction, only response. But you are reacting all the time. There is the judgement for or against, This is right, that is wrong.

The response I am talking about is the physical response to the situation. I function in the physical plane all the time. I am not thinking of anything when I see you. If I turn this side you are wiped out, you are finished for me. There is no mind. If necessary it is recalled, if you ask questions. Reaction is thinking about it "right, wrong, good, evil. Response is just looking without the intervention of thought. Reaction is mental. Response is physical. You are all the time reacting. You are not physically responding to the things out there.

The physical organism knows what to do in a particular situation. So you don't have to think about it. There is no preparation. If there is a snake you step back. It is finished. You don't think about it. Physiological protection is all that this physical organism is interested in, nothing else. The structure which is always thinking of every possible situation, envisaging how to be prepared to deal with each and every kind of situation that might arise during the course of your life, is a thing that has no meaning because every situation is quite different.

Life guides you. I don't want to use the word life because that mystifies the whole thing. This organism is interested in protecting itself and it knows how to survive. When I go for a walk I tell friends, Please, for goodness sake, look, don't think. You don't have to think. Just use your eyes and your ears and they will guide you. The vision becomes extraordinarily clear. The listening mechanism becomes extremely sensitive, that is all. The senses are not deprived of their activity here, they have a field day. They go where they want, think what they want, anything that comes. There is no good thought, no bad thought, no sensual thought, no spiritual thought. All thoughts are the same.

You may ask, How can such a man have a sensual thought? There is nothing he can do to suppress that thought or to give room for that thought to act. This is a reality, a fact. But when these thoughts try to take root there everything in you tightens. You don't have to do a thing. The thoughts cannot stay there. There is no continuity, no build-up. One knows what it is and there it ends. Something else comes up.

But it doesn't end there for you. You say, How can I have these sensual thoughts? You think you are not free if you have sensual thoughts but if you don't have them you can be certain that you are not a living human being. Saint or sinner, one must respond to every stimulus.

* * * * *

You must respond. If there is a woman, there must be a physical response to that. Otherwise, you are a corpse. But here there is no continuity, no build-up. Something else comes up. Thoughts come and go, most of the time you don't even know that they are there. They cannot stay. They are moving. When you recognize there's trouble, fine, it cannot stay there for long. It is pushed out by the next thing. Before you realize what is happening it is gone. When you try to look at it, it is not there. What you are looking at is completely different from what was there before. You don't have to do a thing.

This man is not a stone. He is affected by everything that is happening there. Nor does he bother to create an armor. The religious man has built an armor around himself. Here the cumulative process has come to an end. The only action is physical action, only on that level. The senses are running like wild horses. There is nobody who is controlling them. They run here, there and everywhere as the situation demands.

This action is the movement of life, the real movement of life, and it has no direction. If you accept the helplessness the problem is solved. That is why I say there is no freedom of action for you. It's not a fatalistic philosophy I am talking about but preventing the past from interfering with and coloring the present. All this talk of sublimation of sex energy is bunkum.

I make emphatic statements because it is something I have experimented with before and I know what it is. By conserving sex energy you are not going to improve yourself in any way. It is too silly and too absurd. Why has so much stress been laid on that? Abstinence, continence, celibacy, is not going to help to put you in this state, in this situation. You can have sex today and this kind of thing can happen to you tomorrow. And this can happen even through sex.

If there is a moment there where there is nobody who is experiencing anything "that is the moment when this kind of a thing can happen. It doesn't have to be the discourse of a religious man. Anything that is happening can do the trick because if you don't translate anything that will take care of it.

There is no such thing as sublimation, nothing going up there. It is only going out. But these holy men won't accept it. If they were honest enough they would know what they are saying. Sex is unfortunately separated from other activities. Why I have always wondered. It is one. It can't be separated. Why have they put it on a different level? It is that that has created the problem. Religion is responsible for that. It has created that for us.

The questioning of our actions is really the moral problem. We must have new moral codes of conduct. That is necessary, otherwise we can't function. That is the trouble now. The old codes are all out of date, anachronistic, finished. Who cares about sex? Sex is so easy now. The extraordinary man, as opposed to your ordinary man, has to live here in this society. He cannot run away and live in a cave and meditate.

There is no conflict with this society at all. Although it is so unreal I function in the world accepting the reality accepted by everybody. It is very important. I can't sit in a cave. This is the only reality for such a man. The ultimate reality is bosh and nonsense. It doesn't exist. It's a myth. As long as you are feeling the feelings of society you are part of that society. Because you have no such thing as your own thoughts, your own experiences or your own feelings, you can't run away from this society.

You are not separate from the society. You are the society. You are part of this world. You are affected by it. You are not involved but you are affected. There is a difference between getting involved and allowing yourself to be affected. All the windows are open. It doesn't matter, this or that, anything can come. We have very strange ideas in the religious field, all kinds of funny things.

You are escaping from yourself. What you do or do not do does not matter at all "your practice of holiness, your practice of virtue. That is socially valuable for the society but that has nothing to do with this. The moral codes of conduct have no relationship whatsoever to this. Not that this man is immoral. He cannot be immoral. It is impossible for him, you see. His behavior patterns probably to some extent fall within the framework of the moral and religious code but he's a danger. What I am saying is a threat to you as you know yourself and as you experience yourself.

* * * * *

My point is this; that not because of love but because of the terror of liquidating ourselves we will learn to live together. You cannot hurt anybody without hurting yourself, not psychologically but physically. Only when we realize this will we learn to live together. As long as each individual seeks his own security, there can be no overall security. We are talking of peace in international terms but it has to percolate down to the level of individual relationships.

Only terror will make us live together in peace whether we like it or not. You can take a revolver and make the world's strongest, most powerful man dance for you. It is a fact. This is going to survive somehow. You are not going to let the whole thing blow up. Man has survived for so long and now we are all of a sudden talking about values and all that kind of stuff. What for? It has not helped us to live in harmony.

We have created this moral problem, you see. Plants and animals don't have a religious problem. Man has created this religious problem. You see, this has absolutely no social content at all and I can't think of any collective action. So this individual is just like something thrown out by nature and whether anybody recognizes him or not is of no importance. This man cannot be of any use to this society. I don't have the missionary zeal in me or any desire to save mankind.

I am not in the holy business. I sing my own song. If somebody comes I talk. If nobody comes I go for a walk or look at the birds, look at the trees. So many things are happening. But I don't go out and sit on a platform and talk. I am not cut out for that kind of a thing. I am a simple man. I don't want to complicate things unnecessarily. You see, my position is very simple. I'm always available. I have no private life which I can call my own. Anybody can come at any time. I just see them and say, Good morning, what can I do for you? That's all I can do. I have nothing to give, that's all.

* * * * *

Knowledge is not something mysterious or mystical. You know that you are happy and you have theories about things. This is the knowledge we are talking about. You introduce another knowledge; spiritual knowledge. But spiritual knowledge, sensual knowledge "what is the difference? We give the names to them. Fantasies about God are acceptable but fantasies about sex are called sensual, physical. There is no difference between the two. One is socially acceptable, the other is not. You are limiting knowledge to a particular area of experience so then it becomes sensual and the other becomes spiritual. Everything is sensual to me.

The knowledge that is essential for the living organism "all of that is necessary. But all those speculations about God, truth, reality, have no meaning at all. They are all cultural values. They are totally unrelated to the survival of the living organism. They are all socially, arbitrarily fixed, religious values. All our tastes are cultivated tastes. Likes and dislikes are all cultivated.

There is no such thing as absolute morality. By morality I mean questioning your actions before and after. It is all social. For the smooth running of society these codes are necessary. These religious people have created a policeman inside you. Certain actions are termed good and certain other actions are termed bad either before or after you do them. That hasn't helped you in any way.

It is thinking that has created the problem. Man's problem is basically the moral dilemma "questioning your actions before and after. It has become a neurological problem, not a religious problem. Even God is a neurological problem. God is the jumbled spelling of dog but the whole of your being is reacting to the word God.

All your beliefs, they are not just psychological, they are neurological. You don't know what is good. You know only what is good for you. That's all you are interested in. Everything centers around that; all your art and reason centers around that. I am not being cynical. That's a fact, nothing wrong with it. I'm not saying anything against it. The situations change but it is that which is guiding you through all situations. I'm not saying it is wrong, you see. If it is not so something must be wrong with you. As long as you are operating in the field of what they call the pair of opposites, good and bad, you will always be choosy in every situation. That is all, you cannot help that.

A moral man is a chicken. A moral man is a frightened man, a chicken-hearted man. That is why he practices morality and sits in judgement over others. And his righteous indignation! A truly moral man will never talk of morality or sit in judgement on the morals of others; never. Man is always selfish and he will remain selfish as long as he practices selflessness as a virtue. The basic pleasures you are indulging in I am not against at all. Whatever you do I am not against at all.

There is restlessness because you have an ideal way of doing things, a perfect way of doing things. You think that there is something more interesting than what you are doing. If that is knocked off, what you are doing becomes very interesting.

You have been told that you should practice desirelessness but that is falsifying you. Desire is there. Desire as such can't be wrong, can't be false, because it is there. Anger as such can't be false because anger is there. You are talking of some energy which those people have defined as God or God-knows-what. Don't you see that it is the very thinking that has turned this into a problem? Anger is energy. Desire is energy. All the energy you want is already in operation there. What the hell do you want energy for? You are destroying this energy through thinking. It is only thinking that has created the problem. Without thinking there is no problem. What I'm saying is that through thinking you cannot solve the problem. Thinking can only create problems.

You hope that you will be able to resolve the problem of desire through thinking because of the models of saints who you think have controlled or eliminated desire. If that man has no desire, as you imagine, he is a corpse. Don't believe that man at all! Such a man builds some organization and lives in luxury which you pay for. You are maintaining him. He is doing it for his livelihood. There are always fools in the world who fall for it.

Once in a while he allows you to prostrate before him. You will be surprised if you live with him. You will get the shock of your life if you see him there. That is why they are all aloof, because they are afraid you will catch them some time or the other. The rich man is always afraid that you will touch him for money; so too the religious man. He never comes in contact with you. Seeing him is far more difficult than seeing the president of your country. That is a lot easier than seeing a holy man. He is not what he says he is, what he claims he is. But those men who have made it, they live amongst the people. You can see them always there.

* * * * *

You will never know the truth because it's a movement. You cannot contain it. You cannot express it. It's not a logically ascertained premise. It has to be your discovery. What good is my experience? We have thousands of experiences recorded. They haven't helped you. It's the hope that keeps you going because hope is the structure.

So-called self-realization is the discovery for yourself and by yourself that there is no self to discover. That will be a very shocking thing, I tell you. It's not going to be an easy thing. It's not going to be handed over to you on a gold platter. You have to become completely disillusioned then the truth begins to express itself in its own way. It is useless to try to discover the truth. The search for truth is absurd.

You cannot communicate what you cannot experience. I don't want to use those words because inexpressible and incommunicable imply that there is something which cannot be communicated, which cannot be expressed. There is an assumption that there is something there which cannot be expressed, which cannot be communicated. There is nothing there. I don't want to say there is nothing there because you will catch me; you will call it emptiness, void and all that sort of thing. I can only put it this way "whatever is there cannot be experienced. Whether there is anything there I don't know. I have no way of knowing it at all.

Even assuming for a moment that you are an enlightened man, you have no way of knowing anything about it. It can never become a part of your knowledge. This has understood that it is not possible to experience anything any more. I don't know if I quite make myself clear. The individuality, the isolation, the separation or whatever you want to call it is not there anymore. What separates you, what isolates you, is thought. It creates frontiers, boundaries. Once that is not there you are boundless, limitless; not that you can experience that boundlessness and limitlessness of your consciousness.

The content of your consciousness is so immense that you can't say anything about it. That is why I say it's a state of not knowing. You really don't know. But how do you know that you do not know? It's not that you say to yourself that you do not know but in relation to the ordinary state of consciousness you have no way of knowing that at all; nobody has any way. There is not even an attempt on your part to grasp something. You don't accumulate experiences.

If you want to experience one thing, the whole series of mysteries are there knocking on your door. This is not an experience at all. You are interested in experiencing the ultimate reality "truth, God, God-knows-what" but it's futile for you to attempt to experience a thing which you cannot experience. It doesn't mean that it is beyond the experiencing structure. Rather, the experiencing structure comes to an end. If you don't recognize what you are looking at it means you are not there.

What are you? You are nothing but a bundle of all these experiences, the knowledge you have about them. I see and I don't know what I'm looking at. My sensory perceptions are at their peak capacity but there is nothing inside of me which labels. The knowledge I have about things is in the background. It is not operating.

In a way the whole of life is like a great big dream. I am looking at you but I really don't know anything about you. This is a dream, a dream world. There is no reality to it at all. When the experiencing structure is not manipulating consciousness or whatever you want to call it then the whole of life is a great big dream from the experiential point of view; not from this point of view here but from your point of view.

You see, you give reality to things "not only to objects but also to feelings and experiences" and think that they are real. When you don't translate them in terms of your accumulated knowledge, they are not things. You really don't know what they are. To you, in relation to the reality you give to things, you would call this state of not knowing a dream.

Here there is no such thing as reality any more, let alone the ultimate reality. I function in the world as if I accept the reality of everything the way you accept it. It's like water flowing. When there is an obstacle to the water then there is an action there, either it overflows or it takes a diversion, but here and now when I begin to walk in that direction there is no question of an obstruction or anything there.

* * * * *

Look here "there is no present to the structure of the you. All that is there is the past which is trying to project itself into the future. You can think about past, present and future but there is no future, there is no present, there is only the past. Your future is only a projection of the past. If there is a present, that present can never be experienced by you because you experience only your knowledge about the present and that knowledge is the past. So what is the point in trying to experience that moment which you call now?

The now can never be experienced by you. Whatever you experience is not the now. So the now is a thing which can never become part of your conscious existence and which you cannot give expression to. The now does not exist as far as you are concerned except as a concept. What you experience is only the knowledge you have about it, and the knowledge has come from some outside agency always. It is somebody else's, not yours. Somebody else will come along and take it away. A more persuasive man comes along and says, That's not the way to experience, there's another way, and so on. As I see it, there is no preparation for it "no yoga, no prayers, no meditation. Probably, you will experience anything you want. Thought is something extraordinary.

You have to go through all these experiences. Sometimes out of nowhere something like an experience too extraordinary to have happened to you or anybody ever before is there, but that did not come out of nowhere. It is part of the knowledge of consciousness. All that man has experienced before you is part of consciousness. It is all there. All that is a contamination; anything you experience, however profound it may be, is a contamination. It has nothing to do with this state. Somebody has experienced that before. Anything you experience there is a worthless thing, it is not that. Whatever is experienced is thought-induced. Without knowledge you can't experience and experience strengthens the knowledge. It is a vicious circle" the dog chasing its own tail.

Expansion of consciousness is nothing, but you give so much importance to that. Drugs will make it a lot easier than all these meditations and yogas. There is a sudden blow-up of consciousness and this sudden expansion releases tremendous energy there inside of you. What is the effect of that on the physical body? The physical body responds to what you call the sudden expansion of consciousness. The only way the physical body can respond to that sudden expansion of consciousness is by taking a sudden breath. Suddenly you take a breath and the whole breathing pattern changes. It's breathtaking. You experience such things all the time. There is nothing to these experiences. None of these experiences mean anything.

The realization dawns on you that those experiences, however profound they may be, aren't worth anything, that's all. You may be in a blissful state; even after that calamity you have blissful states, ecstatic states, a sudden melting away of everything that is there. It doesn't mean anything. You experience, I experience" what is the difference?

In India, holy people experience some petty little thing called a blissful state or the absence of body consciousness and they think something marvelous is happening. All those things are limitations. They are limiting consciousness. They are not in any way helping. But to

31

you probably they are of great interest because man is functioning all the time in that limited consciousness. All those religious experiences are no different from the experiences people have when they take drugs.

You cannot experience anything which you can call your own. Whatever you experience, however profound that experience may be, is the result of the knowledge that is part of your consciousness. Somebody must have, somewhere along the line, experienced bliss, ecstasy "call it by whatever name you like" and that experience is part of your consciousness. You have to come to a point where you see that there is no such thing as a new experience at all. The mystic who experiences what the sages have talked about is still in the field of duality, whereas the sages or seers are functioning in the undivided state of consciousness.

The mystic experience is an extraordinary one because it is not an intellectual experience. It helps them to look at things differently, to feel differently, to experience things differently and to interpret the statements of the sages and seers for others. Had it not been for the mystics, the sages would have been clean forgotten long ago. The sages don't depend upon any authority. What they say is the authority. This the sages talked about but the mystics just had experiences. They tried to share that through music and all kinds of things but this is not an experience which can be shared with somebody else. This is not an experience at all.

The mystics are trying to tell you, so they are always in the field of duality, whereas the sage, or seer, or whatever you want to call him, is in the state of undivided consciousness. He does not know that he is a free man so for him there is no question of trying to free others. He is just there. He talks about it and then he goes.

Gaudapada had no disciples. He refused to teach anybody. Ramana Maharshi taught nobody, initiated nobody. Great teachers never use any authority and they do not interpret anyone. The mystics help you to look at things differently, to interpret things differently. You cannot become a sage through any effort. It is not in you hands. A sage cannot have a disciple. A sage cannot have a follower because it is not an experience that can be shared. Even an ordinary experience you can't share with others. Can you tell somebody who has never experienced sex what the sex experience is like?

The sages and seers are original and unique because they have freed themselves from the entire past. Even the mystic experience is part of the past. Not that the past goes for such a man but for him the past has no emotional content. It is not continually operative, coloring the actions. This is the ultimate. You have to totally surrender yourself. It is not surrender in the ordinary sense of the word.

It means there isn't anything you can do. That is total surrender, total helplessness. It can't be brought about through any effort or volition of yours. If you want to surrender to something it's only to get something. That's why I call it a state of total surrender. It's a state of surrender where all effort has come to an end, where all movement in the direction of getting something has come to an end.

All wanting is totally absent. Even the hope must go that some miracle will happen and it will descend upon you from somewhere. All those to whom this kind of thing has happened have really worked hard, touched rock-bottom, staked everything. It does not come easily. It is not handed over to you on a gold platter by somebody. It is a very simple thing, so simple that the complex structure does not want to leave it alone. You seem to know. You imagine. Imagination must come to an end. I don't know how to put it. The absence of imagination, the absence of will, the absence of effort, the absence of all movement in any direction, on any level, in any dimension" that is the thing.

You are interested in experiencing bliss, love, God-knows-what, but that is a worthless thing. If I experience bliss, is that bliss? It is created by the knowledge I have; it is the knowledge. To be free from knowledge is not an easy thing. You are that knowledge "not only the knowledge that you have acquired in this life but the knowledge of millions of years of everybody's experiences. People have some experiences, you see, and on that they build a tremendous superstructure.

The thing is so simple that the complex structure does not want to leave it alone. I don't like the articles written about me. You are trying to present me as a religious man which I am not. You are failing to comprehend the most important thing that I am emphasizing. These articles don't give any idea of what I am expressing.

There is no religious content "there are no mystical overtones at all" in what I am saying. Man has to be saved from the saviors of mankind! The religious people, they kidded themselves and fooled the whole of mankind. Throw them out! That is real courage.

Courage is to brush aside everything that man has experienced and felt before you. You are the only one greater than all those things. Everything is finished. The whole tradition is finished, however sacred and holy it may be. Then only can you be yourself. That is individuality. For the first time you become an individual. As long as you depend upon somebody, some authority, you are not an individual. Individual uniqueness cannot express itself as long as there is dependence. You don't have to depend upon any authority; it has an authority of its own. You will never interpret anything. You will never rely on any authority.

The problem is that even if such a person doesn't talk his very presence becomes a model for somebody. The fact that somebody sits here from morning till evening "what can I do about it? Sometimes they go into trances. They say, How can you deny what is happening to me? And I say, You may do what you like. How can I convince you that I have nothing more than you have? I don't have anything that you don't have.

Your wanting something from somebody is the cause of your misery. The end of illusion is the end of you, so you can't be without illusion. You can only replace one illusion with another. It is very difficult to make you understand the absurdity of the whole search.

I am blocking every escape. Each outlet has to be blocked to put you in a corner. You must be choked to death, as it were. Only a real teacher can find that out and tell you, nobody else. Not those people who interpret the texts; all that is totally unrelated. Only such a man can talk. And such a man never encourages you because he knows that if this kind of a thing has to happen to somebody, that person will not need the help of anybody. In spite of everything it will happen.

Whatever you are doing is blocking its happening. It is misleading to put it that way because there is nothing to happen. You don't realize that whatever you are doing is a self-centered activity. Whatever you are doing in any direction is only strengthening or distorting the whole thing. Spirituality is self-centered activity. It is very difficult to understand that. The instrument that you are using is born in the field of cause and effect. It cannot conceive of anything happening without cause and effect. That is why that is not the instrument, and there is no other instrument.

It is a quantum jump. It jumps from here to there. You cannot link up these things. You put me on the other side of the river. You want to cross in a boat. That boat is a leaky boat and you will sink. There is no other bank and there is no river to cross, no boat. It is very difficult for you to understand that. You have created an image and put the image on the other side. I say, No, for goodness sake, I am on the same bank. There is no river to cross and no boatman is necessary!

Nobody can guide you. You have no guidelines because he himself doesn't know. If I knew, I would guide you along. Such a man cannot guide or lead you anywhere. It is not that I am against gurus, not at all. He knows, even your books say it, that it is not the guru that can help you. It doesn't mean some sort of mysterious thing.

The hymns say, Whomever it chooses, to him it happens. That does not mean that there is any power outside of you. That potential is there in you already. It has the capacity to explode. If through some strange chance, if through some luck, thought remains by itself without splitting itself into two "something has to happen to that. It is like an atomic explosion, not one but trillions. When it explodes it blasts everything that is there. It is a chain reaction. One after the other, every cell is involved.

It is not so easy. Not through logic or power or somebody's teaching can you make it happen, but the possibility of that kind of thing happening is there in everybody because that is its nature. I can't give it to you or tell you how this happened. That is the reason why I say it has no cause and cannot be reproduced. Reproducing a copy has no value at all. That is why it cannot be reproduced. It is not my opinion. No teacher has reproduced another teacher like himself. While he may have followers, he has something which cannot be reproduced because nature does not use anything as a model to reproduce another.

So all your morality and all your practicing this, that and the other has no meaning. That is why the Upanishadic seers never talked of morality or practices whereas the saints have emphasized them because they are second-class imitators. This kind of a thing, if it has to happen, will happen in spite of those things. If anything has to happen it has to happen here and now.

* * * * *

You see, the trouble is that the more beliefs you have the more difficult it becomes for you because one more thing is added to your tradition. Your tradition, which you want to preserve, has been strengthened and fortified by the appearance of a new man because you are trying to fit him into the framework of your tradition. This structure is interested in protecting the tradition. But this is interested in breaking the cumulative nature of the tradition, not in maintaining the tradition but in breaking it.

A certain person breaks it and you make it a part of that accumulated wisdom. That is why it becomes more difficult. Even the revolutionary statement of that particular individual who has achieved this breakthrough has already become part of your tradition. Your very listening has destroyed the revolutionary nature of this breakthrough and has made this a part of knowledge, tradition, because you are the tradition. The listening mechanism that is operating there in you is the tradition. It strengthens itself, fortifies itself, through the listening process.

By the time this has been accepted, the need has been created for somebody else to come and blast it. That is why I am talking. The very expression of this has created the need for something new to happen. That is its nature. That is the purpose, if there is any purpose, not to create a following but to create something new there. Something new is saving you from the burden of the past. The moment it is given expression to, it is old. Why be like those handing over the torch from one person to another and maintaining the hierarchical structure?

Following another is an animal quality. Man cannot become man so long as he follows somebody. What is responsible for man remaining an animal is that culture, the top dog. Following somebody, that has not helped you at all. Why be a cheap imitation of Buddha or whosoever? What for? I tell you, you are far more unique and extraordinary than all those saints and saviors of mankind put together. Why do you want to be a cheap imitation of that fellow? That is one of the myths. Forget it. You have that potential. The first thing is to drop copying others.

* * * * *

Now supposing you are there, let us put it that way. You will not say to yourself or to others that you are a free man. You will not try to free anybody. It is just there like the flower. The wildflower has a beauty of its own. Other flowers are no match to that. It will go one day. It doesn't matter. There is nothing that you can do. That statement has no meaning for you because you are doing something all the time. You have to do something or the other, so this statement has no meaning, no relevance to you at all.

The description of this state is a very dangerous thing because you are trying to relate this to the way you are functioning. Whatever you want you can get, whatever experience you want, but whatever you experience is worthless. Enlightenment, if there is any such thing, is not an experience at all. So this dawns on you, this realization, if you want to put it that way, that there is nothing to realize.

Self-knowledge, or self-realization, is to realize for yourself and by yourself that there is no self to realize. That is going to be a shattering blow to the one pursuing it. That is why it happens to one in a million, one in a billion, not because of what he does or does not do. All your doing is the barrier. Unless you are there you can't understand the meaninglessness of this at all. When you are there you see that the very search is the self, the very thing you want to be free from. There is no you independent of the search; that you don't understand.

It is the goal that you have set before yourself that has created the you. If the goal goes, if you brush aside the goal, you replace one with another. You can't be without illusion. You replace one illusion with another. If illusion goes, you go. If you accept the goal it is alright with me but I say that the goal itself is false. I maintain that there is nothing to be achieved, nothing to be accomplished, nothing to be attained. So all that you are doing to achieve your goal is meaningless. The earlier it dawns on you the better for you. If those things produce some experiences it will be very difficult for you to transcend your own experience.

Somewhere along the line it is bound to dawn on you, you know, that it is not taking you anywhere, but the hope keeps you going, the hope that one day through the same thing you will probably reach your goal, because that instrument is born out of time, is born out of cause and effect, and it cannot conceive of anything except in terms of time. So if time is not there, there is nothing to happen, let alone in the future, because it is time that has created the need for the timeless. Time means the future. If this time is cut off, it is not as if what you expect to happen will happen now. There is nothing to happen here. Time burns itself out when the timeless is knocked off.

Whatever you want to happen is in terms of time. Assuming for a moment that you are already in the blissful state, you don't want to be in that state tomorrow. Whatever the state you want to be in, you are not in that state, because the goal is there, which is tomorrow, not today. So if this is not there, the thought which is thinking in terms of something happening in time is not there. Unfortunately, there is nothing to happen. Happening is in time. When time is not there, there is no happening.

Self is God. The divine you want in the future is already here. There is nothing to happen. Achieving "it doesn't matter what you call it" is in time so it is bound to be caught up in cause and effect. You want to produce a result but this is not a result, not a happening, not an achievement. Anything you do with this will cause you pain. There's no end to that. You will keep searching for this eternally. You are not going to get it. Even if you get what you want and experience bliss, love, God-knows-what, there is always more of it. Silence you experience but you want permanent silence. You want always to be in silence but in the very nature of things there is no permanence at all.

You have never lived with these people. I do not know if there are any. It's a very simple thing. It's so simple that the complex structure does not want to leave it alone. There's nothing that you can do. You can stay with any teacher all your life. Nothing is going to happen. There is no inside or outside, you understand? The triggering apparatus is part of you. It's there. All techniques strengthen the very self you want to be free from. For what are you meditating? You want to be free from something. There is a continuous flow of thoughts and you are linking up all these thoughts all the time.

* * * * *

All meditation is a self-centered activity. I don't talk of a meditative state. This individual is always in a state of meditation. Where is that movement? I am wondering. That is the meditation that is going on. Not that I am wondering in the usual sense of the word. This individual remains in a state of wonder for the rest of his life. Outside and inside are created by thought. When there is no movement of thought you don't know whether it is inside or outside. This is just like a mirror, a live mirror reflecting things exactly as they are.

There is nobody here. I don't see anything. The whole of my body is reflecting things exactly the way they are out there. The recognizing and naming mechanism is in the background except when there is a need for it. This absence of the movement of thought which recognizes and names things is the state of moksha. You imagine that it's something he goes into and comes out of. Not at all, he's always there. Whether the eyes of such a man are open or closed, he does not know what he is looking at. This state is always a state of wonder. He doesn't know what he is hearing, he doesn't know what he is smelling, and yet his senses are working at their peak capacities, extraordinarily sensitive, taking in everything.

There is a constant demand on your part to experience everything that you look at, everything that you are feeling inside, because if you don't do that you are coming to an end. You as you know yourself, you as you experience yourself, are coming to an end, and you do not want that to come to an end. You want the continuity. So all spiritual pursuits are in the direction of strengthening that continuity. It's a self-centered activity. Through self-centered activity how can you be free from the activities of the self? All your experiences, all your meditations, all your prayer, all that you do, is self-centered. It is strengthening the self, adding momentum, gathering momentum, so it is taking you in the opposite direction. Whatever you do to be free from the self also is a self-centered activity.

You can't divide these things into two. The process you adopt to reach what you call being is also a becoming process. I don't know if I make myself clear. There is no such thing as being and becoming. You are always in the becoming process, no matter what you call it. If you want to be yourself and not somebody else, that also is a becoming process. There is nothing to do about this. Anything you do to put yourself in that state of being is a becoming process. That is all that I am pointing out.

Every time you do something, whether it is a good deed or a bad deed, you are strengthening that. You see, we are all functioning in a thought sphere, if I may use that phrase. What you pick out of that is according to your particular background, your culture. This is the product of the culture. You pick up thoughts which are beneficial to you to protect thought. Thought is a protective mechanism. What is it that it is protecting? It is protecting itself. It will do everything possible to prevent itself from breaking up. So even if you introduce the so-called spiritual pursuits it is only the strengthening of that. It is not in the opposite direction so you are on the wrong track.

* * * * *

I am always negating what I am saying. I make a statement but that statement is not expressing all that is being said so I negate it. I negate the first statement, the second statement and all the other statements. That is why sometimes it sounds very contradictory. I am negating it all the time; not with the idea of arriving at any point, just negating. There is no purpose in my talking. I am only pointing out the basic situation that you cannot understand what I am talking about.

It is not possible for you to listen to me without interpreting. I am all the time trying to knock off the reference point. When the reference point is absent, there is no need to understand me. You understand? I am all the time saying that. You won't even know what I am talking about. You are not in a position to accept or reject what I am saying. You accept a statement because it fits your reference point, your assumptions, like self-realization, God-realization, etc. The reference point is you. There is nothing other than the reference point there. That is you. If the reference point goes, you go with it. That is the end of you.

Your very listening is interpretation. You never listen to anybody. It is not possible for you to listen to anybody without interpreting. The interpretation is a part of your background, you see, so it is not possible for you to listen to anything without interpreting what you are listening to.

So is there any other listening? There is a listening quite independent of words, but that is not on the conscious level. It does not mean that you are unconscious. I must make it very clear. That is a pure and simple physical response to the sound. The sound sets in motion the tympanum. So it is just a vibration. You really don't know what he is talking about. This is a physiological phenomenon so I express this only in physiological terms, not in psychological, not in religious, not in spiritual terms, because it's very important for me to express this state in pure and simple physical and physiological terms.

This is just a machine responding to the stimuli of your questions. You have created the problem of their answers, I am not involved. I have no commitment to consistency. I have no viewpoint to put forward, no thesis to expound. I only respond to your stimulus. When you ask a question it is picked up immediately, I don't even decode it. Before you have even asked the question the answer is there. You can do it, it is nothing unusual. If you are not preoccupied with anything of your own it is an easy thing. It is not thought-reading. It is just an echo chamber.

What is going on there is going on here. You can't do that. You want to decode every thought, to translate everything. What I'm saying can't be experienced by you except through the help of thought. In other words, as long as movement of thought is there it is not possible for you to understand what I'm talking about. When it is not there, there is no need for you to understand. In that sense, there is nothing to understand.

Life is one unitary movement, not two different movements. It's moving, it's a continuous flux, but you cannot look at that flux and say, That is a flux. Then why do I say this is a flux? It is only to give you a feel about it that I use those words, but if you translate these words in terms of your concepts and abstractions you are lost. Really, you do not know a thing about what is being said. You don't understand at all. So if you realize that, what happens? Then there is no movement of thought there. Wanting to understand means there is a movement of thought.

You really don't know a thing about what this chap is saying. Then what happens inside of you is only that you repeat these phrases, word by word, without translating them, without interpreting them in terms of your concepts. His talking is just a noise. You are an echo chamber there. That's all that happens. You are not there. When the you is there you are translating.

This is just a pure and simple physiological functioning of the organism. Because there is life, there is a response. The response and the stimulus are not two different movements. You cannot separate the response from the stimulus. The moment you separate the response from the stimulus, there is a division, it is a divisive consciousness that is in operation.

So it is one movement. Thought and life are one interfluent movement. But there seems to be a movement of thought parallel to the movement of life going on in you all the time. There seems to be, otherwise there would be no need for us to sit and talk about this. Listening to me or trying to understand me would not be there. If there were no continuity of thought in you this situation which we have created for ourselves in this room wouldn't exist anymore. You wouldn't want to listen to any chap describing how he is functioning. Why should you? If he is functioning that way, alright, jolly good. Why are you interested in that? Why do you establish any relationship?

As long as you listen to me you are lost. You listen to me because you want to understand what I am talking about, not that it is something abstract or difficult but your understanding is through that instrument and that is not the instrument. The refined, sensitized instrument, you call intuition, but there is no other instrument. If that is not the instrument and there is no other instrument, the logical conclusion from that statement is, Is there anything to understand? There is nothing to understand. That understanding is here somehow. I don't know how it came. That is why I cannot take you there. It has no cause. You are interested in finding out the cause because you want it to happen in you.

So it is not a question of understanding me. It is just not possible to understand. The only thing you can understand is within a certain framework and in relation to a point of reference. You think that the more you listen, the more these things become clear to you, but the clarity of thought is making it more difficult for you to understand what I am talking about. As long as you think that you can see more and more clearly, I say you have seen nothing. If you say you have seen, you have not seen, because seeing is the end of the structure that says that. There is no seeing you can know. In other words, there is no seeing. As long as you think you can understand this more, see the world around you more clearly, I say you will see nothing and understand nothing. The difference between you and me is that you are trying to understand. The absence of what is going on there is what is here. I can only point out the obstacle, that's all.

You see, it is not that I know I am in a state of not knowing. The statement, I don't know a thing, is an expression of that state. Be very clear about it, it is not that I say to myself that I don't know what I am looking at. That state is throwing out the expression. That is the expression, the description, of the state by itself, not that there is somebody who is saying it. The state itself, by itself, says, I really don't know a thing about it.

When all attempts and efforts on your part fail to fit what is being said into the logical framework, the rational framework, I have to say that you cannot in any way understand what it is all about. It is beyond logic. It is beyond rationality. You can never experience it. Don't try! That is not going to help you at all. There are no two ways about it. You, the structure trying to understand, are not going to understand. I can't understand a thing about it. You are still trying to understand, experience, something which you can never understand.

The sages spoke at a time when words had different connotations. Their students listened and passed it on. That is why I often ask, What is my teaching? Please tell me. I don't know a thing about my teaching. I don't know a thing about my state. Not that I can. I know I cannot. The limitation is there. It has its own limitation and it has understood its limitation. It cannot experience that at all, that's all I am saying.

You see, your very listening is an interpretation. You cannot listen to what I am saying. If you are in that state where there is just an echo of what I am saying, repeating the words without understanding them, you really don't know what this chap is talking about and you don't even try to understand. I am telling you the simple fact that you cannot listen to me at all. Whatever you make out of your listening is your own listening, not what I am saying. What I am saying you don't know, I don't know.

What I am saying has no logic. If it has a logic it has a logic of its own, I don't know anything about it. But you have necessarily to fit me into the logical structure of your thought. Otherwise, the logical structure there, the rational thing, comes to an end. You see, you have to rationalize, that is what you are, but this has nothing to do with rationality. It has nothing to do with your logic.

What do you want to understand? There is nothing to understand. That is the understanding I am talking about. If you understand what it is all about, what I am talking about, you are already there. It will be something new, something totally new. You will give expression to it in a completely different way. You will not repeat what Buddha said, what Jesus said, what Rajneesh said or what some other is saying. It will be new and it will express itself in a totally different way. How will it express itself I don't know, you don't know, nobody knows.

* * * * *

If others fit me into their frameworks it is their business. We do not have any vested interest in that. You will probably fit me into some framework and say that so-and-so said this before. That is my misfortune wherever I go. J. Krishnamurti people come, Rajneesh people come, others come, and they say, You are saying the same thing! How the hell do you know I am saying the same thing? Do you know anything of what he is talking about? First of all, you must know what he is talking about and what is there behind it and then you can compare what I am saying with what he is saying.

I am not saying any of those things. I don't compare myself with anybody. Why compare myself with sages, saints and saviors? It would be the biggest tragedy of my life, wouldn't it? I don't compare myself at all. What I am saying is not the same thing that has been said before, no. How do I know? You see, you are trying to fit me into that framework. You have necessarily to do that. If you don't do that you come to an end. That is a dangerous point.

So you have to reject me totally, saying, He is talking some nonsense, rubbish, bosh! Or you have to fit me into whatever particular background you have or into somebody else's framework and say, He is saying the same thing. Otherwise, the tin gods you have created out of somebody's teaching will collapse. You have necessarily to do that, either one or the other.

* * * * *

You are not going to get anything here. You are wasting your time. Pack up and go! That is my message. I have nothing to give. You have nothing to take. If you continue to sit there you are wasting your time. The one thing you have to do is get up and go. If you still think I can give you something you'll have to sit there until kingdom come. I have nothing to give. There's nothing to be given. The holy business, I am not in it. I don't want a thing. I have nothing to give so there's no breach of contract here; nothing. I don't want anything. You may think that I am talking for self-fulfillment. If I do, that will be my tragedy, my misery. So you are out. You are not interested in involving yourself in my tragedy.

I do not give a damn for you. I know you are doomed. If you think something is going to happen and sit here day after day, week after week, year after year, waiting till kingdom come, even then no kingdom will come. Go where you will and do what you want! I tell you very clearly, loud and clear, in clear, unmistakable language, that there is nothing to be communicated now or at any time. I am really surprised, in spite of that assertive statement you hang on here. It is your funeral. You are chasing something which does not exist. There is nothing to be transformed, nothing to be changed, nothing to be understood. So long as you want to be like me you will remain what you are, asking the same questions. You will get the same answer. The one answer for all questions is, Stop asking questions!

* * * * *

The whole culture is built on the foundation of kill and get killed. They are even teaching that. You can't be other than what you are. Whatever you are trying to do to change, you will not succeed. Stop running away from yourself! What is the good of my saying so? There is no use my telling you that because you are not going to stop it. I am telling you to stop it. You are not certain of it, Maybe there is something that can be done.

I am certain that you have no freedom of action. In that sense, I go a step further and say that you are genetically controlled. Naturally, you will say that that statement is a theory. You have a hope that you can do something. There are many people in the holy business who assure you that you can do something, so you will go there, as simple as that. My certainty remains.

Alright, you can go and try your luck. In the end you will find out for yourself and by yourself, That chappie is right! I'll sing my song and go.

On my side it is very clear. There are so many people who have said they can help you but you are not going to get anything from anybody because there is nothing to get. That is why I say that since there is no such thing as enlightenment, the question whether someone is enlightened or not does not at all arise. You are all like-minded people who are after such things, that is all. That is your projection, your ideation, about those people, that is all that I am saying. There may not be anything there other than what you have projected on them.

* * * * *

This is not a thing to be talked about and praised. You are not called upon to change this world. I am not interested in changing the society. What I am saying has absolutely no social content at all. This is an extraordinarily beautiful world! You want to change this world so that you can live in a world of your own ideas. The real problem is that you want to change yourself and find it's impossible so you want to change the world to fit it into your own pattern.

* * * * *

You want to be a good man, a nice man, an innocent man, and all that stuff. You want to be something different, but always in the future. That is what all the teachers promise you, and they just promise, a next life or an afterlife. Till then he is in business, he is assured. If he says there is nothing you leave him. That is why I do not have to bother. You are going to leave in any case because what brings you here will certainly take you somewhere else. You are interested in getting something, some kind of a false hope or promise. Here you are not going to get it.

* * * * *

I don't give false hopes or promises, but religious leaders have created some hope, so you go on and on, like riding a tiger you can't get off. There's no journey. Both are kidding themselves, those who take or pretend to take you on the journey and those who are trying. You can't walk with me. You are so frightened of the thorns there, the stones, you want a trained guide. I myself don't know the terrain. Have you never heard of the proverb that warns you never to walk with a man who has sandals because he always walks on thorns? You will get into trouble. I myself do not know the terrain, I am just going.

* * * * *

This cannot be used to change the world, reform the world, create a new man, a new world "all that is balderdash. Maybe some people do it just to help some people. That's alright, do something. If it works, it works. But to suggest something like that, knowing very well that it is not going to work, is not right, Let's give them some new toys to play with, all the traditional ways have failed.

* * * * *

What are you doing? You are not doing anything. You are repeating new phrases, new words, new idioms. That is all you are doing. You don't accept the fact that all that is a contamination there in that consciousness. Whatever you consider sacred, whatever you consider extraordinary, is a contamination in that consciousness. It has to purify itself. All that "all that dross, all that is holy, all that is sacred" must go. When that has gone you are yourself, otherwise there is dependence.

* * * * *

If religiousness is all you are interested in, there is no need to look anywhere other than organized religion. The profound statements of the great teachers are not much different from each other. All I am saying is that looking to alien lands and religions does not mean anything. You learn new techniques, new systems, new phrases, and then you begin to think and speak in terms of this new language and probably you feel just great but basically it does not mean anything at all.

* * * * *

There is a very powerful plaster. If there is a little crack in your structure you will plaster it over. It is very powerful. It has millions of years of momentum. It knows all the tricks. It can invent any trick to gain momentum. That is its nature. There isn't anything you can do about it. You can discuss it for years but I promise you, you will not get anywhere. If anyone makes you believe you can get somewhere, he's taking you for a ride. There is no one who is honest in this field. No outside agency can help you.

I am not asking you to do anything. How can you be interested in this kind of a thing? What you are interested in is a totally different thing, fancy stuff, fantasy. You may indulge in all kinds of fantasy, that's your affair. If this is not a fantasy, you will be interested in some other kind of fantasy. How can you be interested in liquidating yourself? All that you know "you as you know yourself, you as you experience yourself" is interested in continuity. It knows all the tricks. You cannot beat that. All questions reduce themselves to the one question, "How am I going to get what you have?" And through that a structure is permanently establishing itself there and getting its continuity. There is no "how".

I am not interested in the whole field of self-expression "getting in touch with one's feelings, overcoming inhibitions and so on. I respond to what people come to see me about, the natural state. If people are interested in psychological change, so-called consciousness expansion and all that, let them go to encounter groups or see psychiatrists and engage in what I call the Freudian fraud. In the end, their so-called growth will not bring them happiness. At best, they will simply have learned to be unhappy in a new and richer way. I am not concerned with that. My interest is in the subject they come to see me about in the first place.

My interest is in pointing out the utter impossibility of doing anything whatsoever to attain the natural state. Anyhow, the people who come to see me do not stay very long. They come a few times or hang around for a few months then they either go back to their ordinary lives or go on to some fellow who promises them what they seek. Either way that's fine with me. But one thing I will never do is deceive them. I will never suggest in any way that I can give them anything. I will never hook them into some phony baloney idea about practicing undifferentiated awareness and the observer being the same as the observed and all that.

Everything is okay with me. I am perfectly happy with everything as it is. I am happy with misery, poverty and death. I am also happy with wealth and psychological fulfillment. I think the solution to your real problems is, in any case, not possible for you unless you undergo the sort of biological transformation that has happened to me, which is not to say that I ever consider myself superior to you or to anyone else because of this. Quite the contrary, the idea of superiority or inferiority never even enters my head for one moment. The total absence of this idea is one of the characteristics of this whole transformation business.

* * * * *

The natural state is one in which thinking and life are not two things but one. It is not an intellectual state. It is more like a state of feeling, although I use the word feeling in a different sense than that in which you use the word. It is a state of not seeking. Man is always seeking something "money, power, sex, love, mystical experience, truth, enlightenment" and it is this seeking which keeps him out of his natural state. And although I am in a natural state, I cannot help someone else, because it is my particular natural state, not another's.

So don't listen to me or anybody. Listening to other people is what you've been doing all your life. It's the cause of your unhappiness. You are unique. There is no reason for your wanting to be like another chap. You can't be like him anyway. This wanting "wanting to listen, wanting to understand, wanting to be like such-and-such an individual" has come about because society is interested in creating a perfect man, but there is no such thing as a perfect man. All we can do is be ourselves and no one can help you be that.

You keep listening to someone, it makes no difference whom. And you keep hoping that somehow, tomorrow or the next day, by listening more and more, you will get off the merry-go-round. You listen to your parents and teachers tell you to be good and dutiful and not be angry and so on and that doesn't do any good so you go and learn meditation. You find someone in the holy business and you fall for it. Or perhaps he touches you and you see some light or God-knows-what and you hope he will help you experience enlightenment, but he cannot help you. I do not know if you see the utter helplessness of the situation and how, if anyone thinks he can help you, he will inevitably mislead you. And the less phony he is, the more powerful he is. The more enlightened he is, the more misery and mischief he will create for you.

Life as such has no beginning and no end. It is a beginningless and endless movement and you are only an expression of it. You are conscious of yourself through thought, by which I mean not just conscious thought but that conditioning which transforms the life that passes through you into feelings, into pleasure and pain. And this thought is not yours. It is what you have learned from others. It is second-hand. It belongs to everybody. You belong to everybody. When you accept nature, everything falls into its own rhythm. There is nothing to control and nothing to ask. You don't have to do a thing. You are finished.

* * * * *

You don't let your power express itself. That's something living, vital. It's the throb, the pulse, the beat of life. You are an expression of that life. How can you experience that? This structure of thought through which you experience is dead. It cannot experience that life at all because the one is something living and the other is dead, and there can't be any relationship between the two. You can only experience dead things, not a living thing. Life has to express itself. This is a thing which nobody can teach you. You don't have to get it from somebody. What you have is there. No outside agency can help you; nobody.

So all outside agencies are finished. That is a very difficult point to arrive at. You don't go and listen to anybody no matter how holy he may be. He may be the god of gods, he may say, I have come to liberate the whole of mankind. If you go there just to satisfy your curiosity that's a different matter. You don't seek anything from any source outside so you fall back on yourself and you really don't know.

You want to find out. You ask the question again and again, you are stuck with it, How can I understand this thing? When you are finished with all answers from outside and no answer is forthcoming from inside, what happens to that question? That question cannot remain there, it dissolves itself. Ionization of thought takes place because it cannot escape, and that is energy. That is life.

You can't do a thing. Don't get on this journey of freeing yourself from the conditioning of your own thought. But you are still trying. You accept these ideas. You never question the validity of those statements. It doesn't matter who says it, it is false for you. Not only that, it is falsifying you because you do not test the validity of those statements for yourself. The conditioning, you see, you will never be free from that. Don't believe anybody.

I don't accept that there is such a thing as the mind, let alone the open mind or the unconditioned mind. There is no totality of these thoughts and experiences. They are all disconnected, disjointed things. You'll never be free from thought. If there is any such thing as a thought-less state it can never be experienced by you or by anybody. Whatever you experience there is created by this thought.

* * * * *

It is time that creates the timeless and then pursues it, and through this pursuit time is continuing. Continuity is all that it is interested in. Abstractions are very misleading. If you start talking in terms of innocence, in terms of this, that and the other, you are lost. In that state you really don't know what you are looking at. You don't know that you are looking at your wife. Can there be any relationship? You see, you can talk of innocence but when there is no mind why talk of the innocent mind? Where is the mind or the unconditioned mind? These phrases are very misleading. They are not going to help in any way. To me there is no such thing as mind. Mind is a myth. There is nothing there to be transformed, radically or otherwise.

There is no self to be realized. The whole religious structure that has been built on this foundation collapses because there is nothing there to realize. You can come here. Nothing will happen. Nothing will evolve. You will not get anything from me. That is why I am safe. I live my own life. If somebody comes, I say, Tell me, what can I do? There's nothing much I can do. Thank you. Goodbye.

The very nature of mind is neurotic because it wants two things at the same time. So every individual is neurotic and when you can't get it you become psychotic, you become wild. Not that you necessarily go and beat somebody but you are destroying yourself because the violence is there inside of you. What makes you unhappy is the search for a thing that does not exist. This is the unfortunate situation. You are not getting anywhere. That is not the way at all. Then what is the way? There is no way. Anything I say you turn into a way and add to the momentum. That is not the way. That is not the path. It has to be yours.

All paths must go. As long as you follow somebody else's path, the path is the product of thought. So it is actually not a new path, it's the same old path, and you are playing the same old game in a new way. It is not a new game. It is the same old game that you are playing all the time, but you think you are playing a new game. You have to come to a point where you can't do anything at all.

I say there is no translator who is translating the sensations. There is not even the knowledge that they are sensations. You are translating all these sensations. You can't stop the translation. You are the product of translation. There may not be any stoppage. If somebody says there is a stoppage, To hell with what he is saying, this chap is either a cuckoo or some far out, freaked out ape. He is talking about things that are not real to me. You don't have the courage. You don't want to accept the reality of yourself.

What I am saying is something totally unrelated to the way you are functioning. So then naturally it has to slow down. You don't know. You come to a point where you don't know what to do about the whole business, I can't do anything. This is the only way I know. I don't know any other way. If you see the futility of it all maybe it will not really stop but slow down.

* * * * *

There is nothing to do, nothing to achieve. This is what I have been trying to communicate to those of you who come to see me and who care to listen to me. As long as you want to get or achieve something or want to be enlightened you are not going to be an enlightened. I don't know, I never say to myself, I am an enlightened man, a self-realized man. What does it mean? It doesn't mean anything to me. So to me there's no point in talking about enlightenment or going about with my head raised saying to myself and others, Come ye and listen to me. I am an enlightened man. I am going to liberate you all. That's the holy business.

Maybe you've heard that there is some funny fellow, that he's brutal and is saying all sorts of things. Probably, curiosity brought you here, I don't know. And if you say I do all this for kicks it is alright with me, but I'm not doing it for kicks. Alright, assuming for a moment that I am doing all this for pleasure "why do you allow yourself to be used by me? Keep away! Don't allow yourself to be used by me!

Stay away! My interest is to send you all packing. Don't allow yourself to be exploited by me! I don't get any pleasure. If you don't come tomorrow it's all the same but you don't believe it because the only thing you know is pleasure. I'm not saying there is anything wrong with pleasure. Don't say that it is something wrong. If you accept that you are here for exactly the same reason that a man goes to a bordello, that's going to give you a terrible shock. There's no difference at all.

Perhaps you have heard something about a transformed individual and that is what is bringing you here. This is not born out of thinking. These are just words springing up from their natural source without any thought, without any thought structure.

So take it or leave it! You will be better off if you leave it. Anything you listen to is turned into a method, a system. You want to get something through this. For example, somebody says there is a mind and you must uncondition your mind. How are you going to uncondition your mind? You are conditioning your mind through this lingo. That is all that it is necessary for you to see.

I'll sing this song the rest of my life until I drop dead. Whether anybody listens to it or not is of no importance to me. So, then you leave this chap alone. You never establish any relationship with this man. The moment you use this to get whatever you want to get or to arrive at some kind of a destination you are tricking yourself into the same old game.

There isn't anything you can get from any spiritual discourses or from any religious book. This is what I have been trying to point out to those who care to listen to me. There is nothing to accomplish, nothing to attain. If you are searching for and want anything, the first thing you must do is throw away "lock, stock and barrel, hook, line and sinker" all this stuff that you are hanging on to, otherwise there is no chance for you to be yourself. Any path you follow leads you astray, puts you on the wrong track. If you make anything out of what I am saying you are lost, body and soul, and if there is a God, He must, out of His sheer mercy, save you all and save you from me.

One thing I make very clear, I'm not here to liberate you at all. Who am I to liberate you? What is it that you want to liberate yourself from? You are trying to ask for a thing that you have so I only point out that you're on the wrong track. Your teacher must go. It doesn't matter who it is. What you are reading is the very thing you must be free from.

* * * * *

You are moving away from yourself. You have to be yourself and a path is trying to turn you into something other than yourself. Why do you want to be somebody other than yourself? You see, otherwise you wouldn't listen to anyone. Look here, I want to be full of feeling for everybody. Somebody is talking about love, for example, so you want to be full of that love, whatever it is. You are projecting a hundredfold what you think love is, for example. That's what makes it difficult for you to be yourself.

2. 1982: India, Switzerland and California

This is the only reality I have, the world as it is today. The ultimate reality that man has invented has absolutely no relation to the reality of this world. As long as you are seeking, searching and wanting to understand what you call ultimate reality, or call it by whatever name you like, it will not be possible for you to come to terms with the reality of the world exactly the way it is. So anything you do to escape from the reality of this world will make it difficult for you to live in harmony with the things around you.

We have an idea of harmony, of how to live at peace. There is an extraordinary peace that is there already. What makes it difficult for you to live at peace with yourself is the creation of what you call peace, which is totally unrelated to the harmonious functioning of this body. When you free yourself from the burden of reaching out there to grasp, to experience and to be in that reality, then you will find that it is difficult to understand the reality of anything.

You will find that you have no way of experiencing the reality of anything, but at least you will not be living in a world of illusions. You will accept that there is nothing that you can do to experience the reality of anything except the reality that is imposed on us by the society. We have to accept the reality as it is imposed on us by the society because it is very essential for us to function in this world intelligently and sanely. If we don't accept that reality, we are lost. We will end up in the loony bin.

So we have to accept the reality as it is imposed on us by the culture, by society or whatever you want to call it and at the same time understand that there is nothing that we can do to experience the reality of anything. Then you will not be in conflict with the society, and the demand to be something other than what you are will come to an end. The goal that you have placed before yourself, which you have accepted as the ideal to be reached, and the demand to be something other than what you are, are no longer there.

The pursuit of those goals which the culture has placed before us and that we have accepted as desirable is not there any more. The demand to reach them is no longer there, so you are what you are. When the movement in the direction of becoming something other than what you are isn't there any more, you are not in conflict with yourself. If you are not in conflict with yourself you cannot be in conflict with the society around you. As long as you are not at peace with yourself it is not possible for you to be at peace with others. Even then, there is no guarantee that your neighbors will be peaceful, but, you see, you will not be concerned with that.

When you are at peace with yourself then you are a threat to the society as it functions today. You will be a threat to your neighbors because they have accepted the reality of the world as real and because they are also pursuing some funny thing called peace. You will become a threat to their existence as they know it and as they experience it. So you are all alone. Not the aloneness that people want to avoid. You are all alone.

It's not ultimate reality that one is really interested in, not the teachings of the gurus, not the teachings of the holy men, not the umpteen number of techniques you have, which will give you the energy which you are seeking. Once that movement is not there, that will set in motion and release the energy that is there. It doesn't have to be the holy man's teaching. It doesn't have to be any techniques that man has invented, because there is no friction there. You really don't know what it is.

The movement there and the movement here are one and the same. The human machine is no different from the machine out there. Both of them are in unison. Whatever energy is there, the same energy is in operation here. So any energy you experience through the practice of any techniques is a frictional energy. That energy is created by the friction of thought. The demand to experience that energy is responsible for the energy you experience, but this energy is something which cannot be experienced at all.

This is just an expression of life, a manifestation of life. You don't have to do a thing. Anything you do to experience that is preventing the energy which is already there, which is the expression of life, which is the manifestation of life, from functioning. It has no value in terms of the values we give to whatever we are doing "the techniques, meditation, yoga and all that. I am not against any one of those things, please don't get me wrong, but they are not the means to achieve the goal that you have placed before yourself. The goal itself is false.

If the suppleness of the body is the goal you have before you, probably the techniques of yoga will help you to keep the body supple. But that is not the instrument to reach the goal of enlightenment or transformation or whatever you want to call it. Even the techniques of meditation are self-centered activities. They are all self-perpetuating mechanisms which you use. So the object of your search for ultimate reality is defeated by all these techniques because these techniques are self-perpetuating instruments. You will suddenly realize, or it will dawn on you, that the very search for ultimate reality is also a self-perpetuating mechanism. There is nothing to reach, nothing to gain, nothing to attain.

As long as you are doing something to attain your goal it is a self-perpetuating mechanism. I say self-perpetuating mechanism but I don't mean that there is a self or an entity. I have to use the word self because there is no other word. That is all that it is interested in. Anything you want to achieve is a self-centered activity. When I use the term self-centered activity you always translate it in terms of something that should be avoided because selflessness is your goal.

As long as you are doing something to be selfless you will be a self-centered individual. When this movement in the direction of wanting to be a selfless man is not there, then there is no self and there is no self-centered activity. So it is the very techniques, systems and methods which you are using to reach your goal of selflessness that are self-centered activities. Unfortunately, society has placed that goal before us as the ideal goal because a selfless man will be a great asset to the society, and the society is interested only in continuity, the status quo. So all those values which we have accepted as values that one should cultivate are invented by the human mind to keep itself going.

The goal is what is making it possible for you to continue in this way, but you are not getting anywhere. The hope is that one day, through some miracle or through the help of somebody, you will be able to reach the goal. It is hope that keeps you going, but actually and factually you are not getting anywhere. You will realize, somewhere along the line, that whatever you are doing to reach your goal is not leading you anywhere. Then you will want to try this, that and the other. But if you try one and you see that it doesn't work you will see that all the other systems are exactly the same. This has to be very clear, you see.

Whatever pursuit you are indulging in, somewhere along the line it has to dawn on you that it is not leading you anywhere. As long as you want something you will do that. That want has to be very clear. What do you want? All the time I ask you the question, What do you want? You say, I want to be at peace with myself. That is an impossible goal for you because everything you are doing to be at peace with yourself is what is destroying the peace that is already there. You have set in motion the movement of thought, which is destroying the peace that is there, you see. It is very difficult to understand that all that you are doing is the impediment, is the one thing that is disturbing the harmony, the peace that is already there.

Any movement in any direction, on any level, is a very destructive factor for the smooth and peaceful functioning of this living organism, which is not at all interested in your spiritual experiences. It has no interest in any one of those spiritual experiences, however extraordinary they may be. When once you have one spiritual experience, there is bound to be a demand for more of the same, and ultimately you will want to be in that state permanently.

There is no such thing as permanent happiness or permanent bliss at all. You think that there is because all those books talk of eternal bliss, permanent bliss or permanent happiness. Yet you know jolly well that it is not leading you anywhere. So the mechanism that is involved, the instrument that you are using, is the one that keeps you going, because it does not know anything else. It has come into being through so many years of hard work, effort and will.

Your wanting to be in a state of effortlessness through the use of effort is not going to succeed. So forget about the effortless state. It doesn't exist at all. You want to achieve an effortless state through effort. How the hell are you going to achieve that goal? You forget that everything that you are doing, any movement that is there, any want that is there for whatever reason, is effort.

Effortlessness is something which cannot be achieved through effort. Anything that you do to stop the effort is itself an effort. It's really a maddening thing. You have not really pushed yourself into that corner. If you do, then you will really go crazy. But you are frightened of that. You have to see that everything that you are doing to be in that effortless state, for whatever reason you want to be there, is effort. Even wanting not to use effort also is effort. The total absence of will and effort, all and every kind, may be called an effortless state, but that is not something that you can achieve through effort.

You can change the techniques, you can change the teachers, but basically and essentially the very teaching that you are using to reach your goal is the obstacle. It doesn't matter what teacher you follow. Understanding is the absence of the demand for understanding. It may sound funny to you but that's the way it is. So what do you want to understand? You can't understand me at all. You are not going to understand anything at all. It's not that it is difficult. It is so simple. The complex structure that is involved is the very thing that does not accept the simplicity of it. That is really the problem. It can't be that simple, you think, because that structure is so complex that it doesn't want even to consider the possibility that it could be so simple.

I am not saying anything profound. I have been repeating the same thing day after day. Basically, it sounds very contradictory to you. What I am doing is I make a statement and the second statement negates the first statement. Sometimes you see contradictions in what I am saying. Actually, they are not contradictions. This statement does not express what I am trying to express so the second statement is negating the first statement. The third statement is negating the first two statements and the fourth statement is negating the previous three statements, not with the idea of arriving at any goal, not with the idea of communicating anything to you. There is nothing to be communicated, only this series of negations, not with the idea of arriving at any goal. Your goal is understanding. You want to understand, you see. There is nothing to understand here. Every time you make some sense out of it, I try to point out that is not it.

It is not the doctrine of neti-neti. You know, in India they have evolved this negative approach, but the so-called negative approach is a positive approach because they are still interested in reaching a goal. They have failed through the positive approaches so they have invented what is called the negative approach, Not this, not this. The unknown cannot be reached, you see, nor can it be experienced through the positive approach. The so-called negative approach is not really a negative approach because there is still the positive goal of knowing the unknown or wanting to experience something which cannot be experienced. It's only a trick. That's all it is, playing games.

There is no such thing as the unknown at all. How can I say that there is no such thing as the unknown? How can I make such a dogmatic assertion? You will find out. As long as you are pursuing the unknown, this movement is in operation. There is something that you can do that gives you the hope that maybe one day you will stumble into this experience of the unknown. How can the unknown ever become the known? Not a chance. Even assuming for a moment that this movement is not there, what is there you will never know. You have no way of knowing it at all, no way of capturing and experiencing that or giving expression to it.

* * * * *

To talk of eternal bliss, love "all of that is romantic poetry. You see, if you translate what I am saying in terms of your values, in terms of particular codes of conduct, you are really missing the point. It is not that I am against the moral codes of conduct. They have a social value. They are essential for the smooth functioning of society. You have to have some code of conduct to function in this world intelligently. Otherwise, there will be utter chaos. That is a social problem.

It is not an ethical or religious problem. You have to separate the two things because we are living in a different world today. We have to find another way of keeping ourselves in harmony with the world around us. As long as you are in conflict within yourself, it will not be possible for you to be in harmony with the society around you. You are yourself responsible for that.

If you translate the statements that I am making within the framework of your religious thinking, you are really missing the point. It has nothing to do with religion at all. I am not suggesting that you should change yourself into something other than what you are. It is just not possible. I am not trying to free you from anything. I don't think there is any purpose in this talking. You can brush aside my description and say it is nonsense. That's your privilege. But maybe it will occur to you that the image you have of your goal, or the image of what you are going to do one day, through all the effort and will which you are using, has absolutely no relationship whatsoever with what I am describing. What I am describing is not really what you are interested in.

I wish I could give you just a glimpse of it, a touch of it. You wouldn't want to touch this at all. And what you want, what you are interested in, doesn't exist. You can have a lot of petty experiences if that is what you are interested in. Do all the meditations. Do everything you want. You will have lots of them. It's a lot easier to experience those things by taking drugs. I am not recommending drugs but they are the same. Doctors say that drugs will damage the brain but meditation will also damage the brain if it is done very seriously. They have gone crazy, jumped into rivers and killed themselves. They did all kinds of things, locked themselves up in caves because they couldn't face it.

You see, it is not possible for you to watch your thoughts. It is not possible for you to watch every step you take, it will drive you crazy. You can't walk. That's not what is meant by this idea that you should be aware of everything, watch every thought. How is it possible for you to watch every thought of yours, and for what do you want to watch your thoughts? What for, control? It's not possible for you to control. It is a tremendous momentum.

When you succeed in your imagination that you have controlled your thoughts and experienced some space between those thoughts, or some state of thoughtlessness, you feel that you are getting somewhere. That is a thought-induced state of thoughtlessness. The fact that you experience the space between two thoughts, the thoughtless state, means that the thought was very much there.

It surfaces afterwards, like the Rhone, which flows through France, disappears, and then comes up again. It has gone underground. The river is still there. You can't use it for purposes of navigation, but ultimately it comes up again. In exactly the same way, all these things which you are pushing down into the subterranean regions, feeling that you are experiencing something extraordinary, surface again. And then you will find that those thoughts are welling up inside of you.

You are not aware that you are breathing now. You don't have to be conscious of your breathing. Why do you want to be conscious of your breathing? To control your breathing, to expand your lungs, to do what you like with your chest, that's a different matter. But why do you want to be aware of the movement of breath from the origin to the end? You suddenly become conscious of your breathing. Your breath and thought are very closely related. That's why you want to control your breath. And that, in a way, is controlling the thought for a while. But if you hold your breath for long it is going to choke you to death in exactly the same way that anything you do to hold or block the flow of thoughts is going to choke you to death, literally to death, or damage something. Thought is a very powerful vibration, an extraordinary vibration. It is like an atom. You can't play with those things.

You are not going to reach your goal of completely controlling your thought. Thought has to function in its own way, in its disconnected, disjointed way. That is something which cannot be brought about through any effort of yours. It has to fall into its normal rhythm. Even if you want to make it fall into a normal rhythm, you are adding momentum to that. It has a life of its own which has, unfortunately, established a parallel life within the movement of life. These two are always in conflict. That will come to an end only when the body comes to an end.

Thought has become the master of this body. Thought has totally mastered the whole thing. It is still trying to control everything that is there. You don't have to do a thing. You are not separate from that, that's all I am emphasizing. You cannot separate yourself from the thought and say, These are my thoughts. That is the illusion you have, and you cannot be without any illusion. You always replace one illusion with another illusion; always.

You accept that you are always replacing one illusion with another illusion, so your wanting to be free from illusion is an impossibility. That itself is an illusion. Why do you want to be free from illusions? That's the end of you. It's not that I am frightening you, I am just pointing out that it is not just a lighthearted game to play. That is you, you as you know yourself. When that knowledge you have of yourself is not there any more, the knowledge you have about the world also is not there any more, it can't be there any more. It is not going to come to an end that easily. It will always be replaced by another illusion.

You don't want to be a normal person. You don't want to be an ordinary person. That is really the problem. It is the most difficult thing to be an ordinary person. Culture demands you must be something other than what you are. That has created a certain momentum, a powerful movement of thought. You can use it to achieve something, otherwise it has no use. You can build a tremendous philosophical structure of thought, but that has no value at all. You can interpret any event, but thought is not intended for that. At the same time, you forget that everything you have around you is the creation of thought. You are yourself born out of thought, otherwise you would not be here at all. In that sense it has value. Yet it is the very thing that destroys you. That's the paradox.

Everything that you have created in this world has become possible through the help of thought, but unfortunately, that very thing has become the enemy because you are using thought for purposes for which it is not intended. It can be used for solving the technical problems very well and efficiently but it cannot be used to solve the problems of life. Anything that does not suggest your positive thinking you call it negative. But positive and negative are only in the field of your thinking. When the thought is not there it is neither positive nor negative. As I was saying, there is no such thing as a negative approach at all. It's a gimmick.

* * * * *

I am telling you to stand on your own. You can walk. You can swim. You are not going to sink. That's all that I can say. As long as there is fear, the danger of your sinking is almost certain. Otherwise, there is a buoyancy there in the water that keeps you afloat. The fear of sinking is the very thing that makes it impossible for you to let the movement happen in its own way. You see, it has no direction. It is just a movement with no direction. You are trying to manipulate and channel that movement along a particular direction so that you can have some benefits. You are just a movement without a direction.

* * * * *

There is no inside or outside. What's there is only the operation, the flow of the knowledge. You have gathered all this knowledge from various sources. It gives you power. Knowledge is power. To acquire more and more knowledge, more than is essential for the survival of the living organism, is to acquire power over others.

The technical knowledge that you need to make a living is understandable. You may have to learn a skill. The society is not going to feed you unless you give something in return. You have to give them what they want, not what you have to give.

You have, through ideation and mentation, created your own thoughts which you consider to be yours, just as when different colors are mixed into various hues, but all of them can be reduced to the seven basic colors found in nature. What you think are your thoughts are actually just combinations and permutations of the thoughts of others.

You cannot conceive of the possibility of understanding anything except in time. Everything takes time. It has taken so many years for you to be where you are today and you are still striving and struggling to reach a higher plateau, higher and higher. That instrument which you are using cannot conceive of the possibility of understanding anything without effort, without striving, without producing results, but the issues that you have to deal with in life are the living issues. Thought has not helped us to solve those problems. Temporarily, you can find some solution, but that creates another problem, and it goes on and on. These are all life issues, but the mind is a dead instrument and cannot be used to understand anything living.

How can you bring about a change in consciousness, which has no limits, which has no boundaries, which has no frontiers? You can do every kind of research to find the seat of human consciousness, but there is no such thing as the seat of human consciousness at all. You can try but the chances of succeeding in that are slim.

There is no such thing as a seat located in any particular individual. What there is, is thought. Whenever a thought takes its birth there, you have created an entity or a point, and in reference to that point you are experiencing things. Every time a thought is born you are born. Thought, in its very nature, is short-lived. This state cannot be described in terms of bliss, love, compassion and all that poetic nonsense and romantic stuff because you have no way of experiencing what is there between these two thoughts.

The world you experience around you is also from that point of view. There must be a point and it is this that creates the space. If this point is not there, there is no space, so anything you experience from this point is an illusion. Not that the world is an illusion "the world is not an illusion" but anything you experience in relationship to this point, which itself is illusory, is bound to be an illusion, that's all. The Sanskrit word maya does not mean illusion in the same sense in which the English word is used. Maya means to measure. You cannot measure anything unless you have a point. So if the center is absent there is no circumference at all. That is pure and simple basic arithmetic. This point has no continuity. It comes into being in response to the demands of the situation. They create it.

There is light. If the light is not there, you have no way of looking at anything. The light falls on that object and the reflection of that light activates the optic nerves which in turn activate the memory cells. When the memory cells are activated, all the knowledge you have about that object comes into operation. It is that process which is happening there that has created the subject and the subject is the knowledge you have about it. When you reduce it to that, you feel the absurdity of talking about the self. The lower self, the higher self and self knowing, self-knowledge, knowing from moment to moment, is absolute rubbish, balderdash! You can indulge in such absolute nonsense and build up philosophical theories but there is no subject there at all, at any time.

So not only the I but all the physical sensations are involved in this. Sound, smell and the sense of touch "the operation of any one of these sensations necessarily creates the subject. It's not one continuous subject which is gathering all these experiences, piling them up together and then saying, This is me, but everything is discontinuous and disconnected. The sound is one. The physical seeing is one. The smelling is one. They come and go. There is no permanent entity there at all. What is there is only a first person singular pronoun, nothing else. If you don't want to use that word it is your privilege. That's all that is there. There is no permanent entity there at all.

While you are living, the knowledge that is there does not belong to you. So why are you concerned as to what will happen after what you call you is gone? The physical body is functioning from moment to moment because that is the way the sensory perceptions are. To talk of living from moment to moment by creating a thought-induced state of mind has no meaning to me except in terms of the physical functioning of the body.

When thought is not there all the time, what is there is living from moment to moment. It's all frames, millions of frames, to put it in the language of film. There is no continuity there. There is no movement there. Thought can never capture the movement. It is only when you invest a thought with motion you try to capture the movement, but actually thought can never capture any movement that is there around you. The movement of life out there is the movement of life here. They are together always.

So thought is essential only for the survival of this living organism. When it is necessary it is there. When it is not necessary the question of whether it is there or not is of no importance at all. You cannot talk of that state in a poetic, romantic language. And one in that state won't be hiding somewhere. He will be there shining like the star. You can't keep such people under a bushel. To be an individual is not an easy thing, you see. That means you are very ordinary. You want to be something other than what you are. To be yourself is very easy. You don't have to do a thing. No effort is necessary. You don't have to exercise will. You don't have to do anything to be yourself, but to be something other than what you are you have to do a lot of things.

* * * * *

When there is an actual physical danger, the danger of the extinction of your physical body, then everything that it has as its resource gets thrown into that situation and the body tries to survive in that particular moment. Have you ever noticed that when there is a real physical danger your thinking mechanism is never there to help you? You can plan ahead for every possible situation and be prepared to meet every kind of situation in your life, but actually when there is a physical danger all your planning and all that you have thought about to be prepared to meet every kind of danger and every kind of situation is just not there. The body has to fall back on its own resources.

This living organism is not interested in its continuity in terms of years. This is functioning from moment to moment. The sensory perceptions function from moment to moment. There is no continuity in your physical seeing. There is no continuity in your physical hearing. There is no continuity in your smelling. There is no continuity when you eat something. There is no continuity in the sense of touch. They are all disconnected and disjointed. But thought, in its interest to maintain itself and to continue without any interruption, demands these experiences all the time. That is the only way it can maintain its continuity. The body functions in a completely different way and it is not interested in the activity of thought.

The only thought that is necessary for this body is the thought that it has to use for the survival of the living organism. Even if you do not feed this body, it is not concerned about that. It has certain resources which you have built up through years of eating it falls back on. At the same time, it is foolish not to feed the body hoping that you will attain some spiritual goals. That's what they do in India, they put the body through all kinds of stresses and strains, torture it, because they feel that through this endurance they will be able to achieve whatever their spiritual goals may be.

There is nothing that you can do to make this happen through any will of yours, through any effort of yours, through any volition of yours. If this kind of a thing happens, it is not something mysterious. Thought falls into its natural rhythm of discontinuous and disconnected functioning, that's all. That's all that is there.

Thought will be in harmony with the sensory perceptions and the activity of the senses. There is no conflict there. There is no struggle there. There is no pain there. There is a harmonious relationship between the two. Whenever there is a need for thought, it is always there to act. The action that this body is interested in is only the action that is essential for the survival of the living organism.

Culture has been adopted and accepted as a means of survival, that's all. The society is interested only in fitting every individual into its framework and maintaining its continuity. I don't know if I have made myself clear. The reason why I am emphasizing the physical aspect is not with the idea of selling something but to emphasize and express what you call enlightenment, liberation, transformation, in pure and simple physical and physiological terms. There is absolutely no religious content to it, and no mystical overtones or undertones to the functioning of the body. Unfortunately, for centuries the whole thing has been interpreted in religious terms and that has caused misery for us all.

I am not interested in propagating this. This is not something which you can make happen, nor is it possible for me to create that hunger which is essential to understand anything. I am repeating this over and over again but repetition has its own charm. You are assuming that you are hungering for spiritual attainments and you are reaching out for your goals. Naturally, there are so many people in the market place, all these saints, selling all kinds of shoddy goods. They say it is for the welfare of mankind and that they do it out of compassion and all that kind of thing.

What I am trying to say is that you are satisfied with the crumbs they throw at you. They promise that one day they are going to deliver to you a full loaf of bread. That is just a promise. They cannot deliver the goods at all. There is no use waiting for something to happen to satisfy your hunger. The hunger has to burn itself up. Literally, it has to burn itself out.

It is not because of what you do or what you do not do that this kind of a thing happens. And why it happens to one individual and not another, there is no answer to that question. I assure you that it is not the man who has prepared himself or purified himself for whatever reason to be ready to receive that kind of a thing. It is the other way around. It hits but it hits at random. That is the way nature operates, lightning hits you somewhere. It is not interested in whether it is hitting a tree that is blooming or if it has fruits and is helping the people by providing shade, etc. It just strikes at random. In exactly the same way, it happens to a particular individual.

There are so many things happening in nature which cannot be attributed to any particular cause. So your interest in studying the lives or the biography of some of those people whom you think were enlightened, or godmen, or some such thing, is to find a clue as to how it happened to them so that you can use whatever technique they used and make the same thing happen to you. That is your interest. Those people are giving you techniques, systems and methods which don't work at all. They create the hope that somehow, through some miracle, one day it is going to happen to you, but it will never happen. That is something which you cannot make happen. It is not in your hands.

You are waiting for something to happen tomorrow. Tomorrow nothing will happen. Whatever has to happen, that has got to happen now. And the possibility of that happening now is practically and well nigh impossible because the instrument which you are using is the past. Unless the past comes to an end, there can't be any present. And that present moment is something which cannot be captured by you, cannot be experienced by you. Even assuming for a moment that the past has come to an end, you have no way of knowing that it has come to an end. Then there is no future for you at all.

You have tried but even those who are burning with hunger find it's impossible. Whenever such a thing has happened it happened to those people who had given up completely and totally all their search. That is an absolute requisite for that kind of a thing. The whole movement has to slow down and come to a stop. But anything you do to make it stop is only adding momentum to it. That's really the crux of the problem.

What you are interested in doesn't exist, it's your own imagination based upon the knowledge you have about those things, and so there is nothing that you can do about it. You are chasing something that does not exist at all. I can say that until the cows return home "I don't know when they return home here" or till the kingdom come, but that kingdom will never come.

When enlightenment comes it wipes out everything. That is something which cannot be made to happen through your effort or through the grace of anybody, through the help of even a god walking on the face of this earth claiming that he has specially descended from wherever for your sake and for the sake of mankind. That is just absolute gibberish. Nobody can help you. Help you to achieve what? That is the question, you see.

As long as your goal is there, these persons, their promises and their techniques will look very attractive to you. There is not anything you must do. You have nothing to get here. I have nothing to give you. I am not anything that you are not. You think that I am something different. The thought that I am different from others never enters my head; never. Whenever they ask questions I feel, Why are these people asking these questions? How can I make them see? I still have some trace of illusion maybe I can try. Even that try has no meaning to me. There's nothing that I can do about it. There is nothing to get "nothing to give and nothing to get. That is the situation.

If you want anything, the one thing that you will do is to set in motion the movement of thought to achieve your goal. Anything you make happen has no meaning at all. Then you will want more experiences and then when you succeed in having them you will demand some kind of a permanent situation, permanent happiness, permanent bliss. Yet there is no such thing as permanence at all.

* * * * *

You have no way of knowing what you are at all. Knowing what is there is impossible. That is always related to what you want to be. What you see here is the opposite of what you would like to be, what you want to be, what you ought to be, what you should be. What do you see here? You want to be happy so you are unhappy. Wanting to be happy creates the unhappiness. What you see here is the opposite of your goal of becoming happy, of wanting to be happy. Wanting to have pleasure all the time creates the pain here. So wanting and thinking, they always go together. They are not separate. Anything you want creates pain because you begin to think. If you don't want a thing in this world, there is no thinking. That does not mean thoughts are not there.

Whether you want to achieve material goals or spiritual goals it really doesn't matter. I am not saying anything against wanting. The fulfillment or non-fulfillment of the want is possible only through thinking, so the thinking has really created the problem for you. What I am suggesting is that all the problems we have cannot be solved on psychological and ethical levels. Man has tried for centuries to solve them but he has failed. What keeps him going is the hope that one day, by doing more and more of the same, he will succeed. But the body, as I was saying, has a way of resolving these problems because it cannot take them. The sensitivity of the sensory perceptions is destroyed by whatever you are doing to free yourself from whatever you want to be free from.

The nervous system has to be very alert for the survival of this living organism. It has to be very sensitive. Your sensory perceptions have to be very sensitive. Instead of allowing them to be sensitive you have invented what is called the sensitivity of your feelings, the sensitivity of your mind, the sensitivity towards every living thing around you, the sensitivity to the feelings of everybody that is there, and this has created a neurological problem.

* * * * *

Society is interested in the status quo. It doesn't want to change. The only way it can maintain the status quo or the continuity is through the demand that everybody should fit into its structure, whereas every individual is unique. Nature is creating something unique all the time. It is not interested in a perfect man. It is not interested in a religious man. We have placed before man the goal or the ideal of a perfect man, a truly religious man. So anything you do to reach that goal of perfection is destroying the sensitivity of this body. It is creating violence here. It is not interested in that.

Whatever man experiences "self-awareness, self-consciousness" he has sown the seeds of his total destruction. All those religions have come out of that divisive consciousness in man. All the teachings of those teachers will inevitably destroy mankind. There is no point in reviving all those things and starting revivalistic movements. That is dead, finished. Anything that is born out of this division in your consciousness is destructive is violence. It is so because it is trying to protect not this living organism, not life, but the continuity of thought. And through that it can maintain the status quo of your culture or whatever you want to call it, the society. The problems are neurological. If you give a chance to the body it will handle all those problems, but if you try to solve them on a psychological level or on an ethical level you are not going to succeed.

* * * * *

Any energy that you create through thinking is destructive for the body. Energy cannot be separated from life here. It is one continuous movement. So all the energies you experience as a result of playing with all those things are not of any interest to the smooth functioning of this living organism. They are disturbing the harmonious functioning of this body, a very, very peaceful thing.

The peace there is not this inane dead silence you experience. It's like a volcano erupting all the time. That is silence. That is peace. The blood is flowing through your veins like a river. If you tried to magnify the sound of the flow of your blood you will be surprised. It's like the roar of the ocean. The sound of the beat of your heart is something. You create some funny experience called the experience of the silent mind which is ridiculous, absurd. That is the silence that is there" the roar of an ocean.

The body is not interested in your practices or silences. It has no interest in your moral dilemma or whatever you want to call it. It's not interested in your virtues or vices. As long as you practice virtues so long you will remain a man of vice. They go together. If you are lucky enough to be free from this pursuit of virtue as a goal, along with it the vice also goes out of your system. You will remain a man of violence as long as you follow some idea of becoming a non-violent, kind, soft, gentle person. A kind man "a man who is practicing kindness and virtue" is really a menace, not the violent man.

Somewhere along the line culture has put the whole thing on the wrong track by placing before man the ideal of a perfect man, the ideal of a truly religious man. The religious experience is born out of this division in his consciousness which is not its nature. Luckily, animals don't have this division in their consciousness, except the division that is essential for their survival. Man is worse than an animal, for anything that is born out of thought is destructive; not only destructive to the body but progressively destructive, moving in the direction of destroying everything that man has built for himself.

Religion is not going to save man; neither atheism nor communism nor any of those systems. Not only the teachings but the teachers themselves have sown the seeds of this violence that we have in this world. You can't put them on a pedestal and say that they should be exonerated. The man who talked of love is responsible because love and hate go together. So how can you exonerate them? Why do you want to revive religion? What for? I am not condemning any particular thing. All are responsible for that. Talk of love is one of the most absurd things. There must be two. Wherever there is a division there is this destruction. Kindness needs two. You are kind to somebody or you are kind to yourself. There is a division there in your consciousness. Anything that is born out of that division is a protective mechanism and in the long run it is destructive.

Thought is trying to protect itself. That is why it is interested in continuity. The body is not interested in protecting itself. Whatever intelligence is necessary for the survival of the body is already there. The jungle we have created through our organizations needs that intellect, the intellect that we have acquired through our studies, through our culture, through the whole lot. It has a parallel existence of its own and it is interested in a different kind of survival because there is no end to the life here. This is only an expression of life. If you and I go, life goes on.

Those lights go off but the electricity continues. Something else will come. It is not interested in man. Mankind, unfortunately, has such destructive powers which have originated in its past experience. So the talk of wanting to look at himself, to understand himself, is a divisive movement in man born out of that self-awareness. That's the foundation upon which the whole psychological structure is built.

There is a disturbance in the metabolism of the body brought about through drugs, or through meditation, or through any of those systems and techniques man has invented. You can experience the oneness of life and unity of life. Look at India, which preaches the unity of life and the oneness of life. There you have an example. They are all great metaphysicians, philosophers, everlastingly discussing these things, but it doesn't operate in the lives of the people.

Understanding is dualism. If that division is not there, there is nothing to understand. You can talk of intuition. You can talk of a thousand other things. They are all sensitized thoughts. Your understanding of anything is only for the purpose of changing what is there. You begin to think differently and you begin to experience differently but basically there is no change there.

Your wanting to understand anything is only for the purpose of bringing about a change there. And at the same time you do not want the change. That has created the neurotic situation in man, wanting two things, change and no change. That is the conflict that is there all the time. Something there determines that all is not right. That's why you want to bring about a change. And who is responsible for that demand to change? Culture, society, has placed the demand before you; namely, that you should be like that, you ought to be like that. You understand? So you have accepted that as a model for yourself.

There is no inner and outer. What I am trying to say is that there is a feeling, there is a demand, that there is something more interesting that you can do with yourself, more meaningful, more purposeful, than your existence is today. That is the demand, you see. That is why there is this restlessness. You become restless because of this drive in you which is put in there by the society or culture that makes you feel that there is something more interesting, more meaningful, more purposeful, that your life can be than what it is today. Your naturalness is destroyed by that demand which is put in there by the culture. So then, your life looks meaningless to you if that is all that you can do. You have tried to fill in that boredom with everything possible. You have all these gimmicks" yoga, meditation and all the psychology.

Your naturalness is something that you don't have to know. You just have to let that function in its own way. Your wanting to know that demands some know-how which you want from somebody. The functioning of the heart is a natural thing. The functioning of all the organs in your body is very natural. They are not for one moment asking themselves the question, How am I functioning? The whole living organism has this tremendous intelligence which makes it function in a very natural way.

You are not acting in a natural way because the ideal that has been placed before you by the culture has falsified the natural actions here. You are frightened of acting in a natural way because you have been told the way you should act. The things that are there are running very smoothly and mechanically. You don't have to do a thing about them. The more you try the more resistance you create.

I am not giving you another gimmick or suggesting anything. I just want you to look at this, what you are doing to yourself, not to free you from something and take you away from that because I have some new product to sell. Not at all, I have no new products to sell nor am I interested in selling anything. We just happen to be here, all of us, for some reason or the other. Ultimately, what I am emphasizing all the time is, Look here, there is nothing to understand. When that is understood, that there is nothing to understand, all these conversations become meaningless. So you get up and walk away once and for all. I say, Nice meeting you and goodbye. If the question of how to be happy is dropped, then you begin to live, you see, not bothering about happiness at all. The more you want it, the more you search for it, the more unhappy you remain. They go together, you see.

All the positive approaches that man has invented and used for centuries, they have not resulted in anything useful. They have not produced the results you have been promised. And yet, you go on and on hoping that somehow, through some miracle, you will be able to achieve your positive goals, or the goals which are placed before us through the positive approach. You keep doing it only because you have hope and it is that hope that keeps you going. Don't be caught up in this structure of thought which always suggests the positive and negative. Your goals are always positive. Since your goals have failed to give the desired results, you have begun to look at these things and approach them in a negative way. The positive and negative approaches function only in the field of thought.

Your positive approach so far has not given you the desired results and I am telling you why. I am telling you why you are stuck where you are stuck. But immediately you turn around and say, "Your approach is negative." It is not at all negative. I am presenting the other side to neutralize your argument, not to win you over to my point of view or to stress the negative approach to problems. Your goal being a positive goal, no matter what approach you adopt it is a positive approach. You may call it a negative approach but it is still a positive approach. So you must be very clear about the goal. What I am trying to emphasize is that the goal must go.

The goal which you have placed before yourself has no meaning at all because it has resulted only in struggle, pain and sorrow. You are using will, as I said a while ago, and the will has a certain limitation. You can't use it beyond a certain limit. The use of your will and the use of your effort gives you a sort of additional energy to tackle these problems and to face these problems but actually it is limited in its scope. The energy that you produce is only a frictional energy. The will creates friction and that friction gives you some sort of energy but that energy cannot last long and so you are back again in square one.

All civilizations, all cultures, place before you a goal, whether material or spiritual. There are ways and means of achieving your material goals but even in this respect there is a lot of pain, there is a lot of suffering. And you have superimposed on that what is called a spiritual goal. Christianity, for example, is built on the foundation of suffering as a means to reach your goal. What you are left with is only the suffering and you make a great big thing out of suffering. And yet, you are not anywhere near the goal, whatever is the nature of your goal, whereas in the material world the goal is something tangible.

The instrument which you are using to achieve your material goal does produce certain results. By using that more and more you can achieve the desired results but there is no guarantee. The instrument which you are using is limited in its scope. It is applicable only in this area. So the instrument which you are using to achieve your so-called spiritual goals is the same instrument. You do not realize that all the spiritual goals that are superimposed on your so-called material goals are born out of your fantasy because you have divided life into material and spiritual. It doesn't matter what instrument you use to achieve your goal. Whether it is material or spiritual it is exactly the same.

I want you to be very clear about the goal. What do you want? It is not the want that is wrong but the only way you can achieve your material or spiritual goals is through an instrument. What I am suggesting is that the only instrument you have is thinking. See, one wants to be a millionaire, and a millionaire wants to be a billionaire. That is the goal. A happy man would never want to be happy. He wants to be more and more happy or he wants to be permanently happy.

Sure, you are happy sometimes and you are unhappy some other times. So you want pleasures and you want those pleasures to be permanent. And at the same time, you also know that the so-called demand for pleasure, temporary or otherwise, is giving you pain as well. The goal of every person in this world is exactly the same. What he wants is to have pleasure, not pain "to be happy, not unhappy. What he is actually struggling and striving hard for is to achieve this impossible goal of having one without the other.

If you achieve all the goals you have placed before yourself "success, money, name and fame, position or power" you are happy. In this process, you are struggling hard. You are putting a lot of will and effort into that. As long as you succeed, you have no problems at all. You cannot always succeed. You know all that but there is somehow the hope that it will be possible for you to always succeed. You are frustrated because you find that you cannot always succeed yet there is still hope. Whether it is for material goals or spiritual goals, the demand is to succeed in your efforts to reach, attain or accomplish whatever goals you have placed before yourself.

* * * * *

The body cannot take any sensation, be it pleasurable or painful, for long. It will destroy the sensitivity of the sensory perceptions and the sensitivity of the nervous system. The moment you recognize a particular sensation as a pleasurable sensation, naturally there is a demand to make that pleasurable sensation last longer. So every sensation, depending upon the intensity of that sensation, which is plagued by you to invest it with more intensity or less intensity, has a limited life of its own.

The demand comes only when you separate yourself from that pleasurable sensation and begin to think of how you can extend the limits of the pleasurable sensation or the moments of happiness. Your thinking has turned that particular demand to make this pleasurable sensation last longer than its natural duration into a problem. It has turned that into a problem for the functioning of this body and by so doing it has created a neurological problem. It is doing everything possible to absorb that, whereas your thinking makes it impossible for this body to handle that in its own way for the simple reason that you are trying to solve those problems within the field of your religious or psychological approaches.

Actually, those problems are neurological problems and if the body is left alone to handle them in its own way it will do a better job than your trying to solve them on psychological or religious levels. All the solutions that we have been offered and which we have been adopting for centuries have not done any good except to give us a little bit of comfort to help you bear the pain. When this understanding dawns on you, then you will realize that the energy that is there in the body, which is the manifestation of life or expression of life, handles everything in a tremendously easier way than the frictional thinking which you are generating through your ideas of how to handle these problems.

You are creating the problems but actually you are not looking at them at all. You are not dealing with them. You are more interested in solutions than the problems. That makes it difficult for you to look at the problem. I am suggesting that, Look here, you don't have any problems.

You are not interested in solving the problem because that will put an end to you. You want the problems to remain. You want the hunger to remain because if you are not hungry you will not seek this food from all these holy men. What they are giving you are some scraps, bits of food, and you are satisfied. Even assuming for a moment that he can give you the whole loaf of bread, which he cannot do, he will only promise to keep it here hidden somewhere. Bit by bit he gives you and thereby you are not dealing with the problem of hunger. But you are more interested in getting a bit more from that fellow who is promising you a solution rather than dealing with your problem of hunger. You are more interested in getting some more crumbs from that fellow.

You never look at the problem. What is the problem? Anger, for example "where is that anger? Can you separate the anger from the functioning of this body? It's like a wave in the ocean. Can you separate the waves from the ocean? You can sit there and wait until the waves subside so that you can have a swim in the ocean, like King Canute, who sat there for years and years hoping that those waves in the ocean would disappear so that he could have a swim in a calm ocean. That will never happen. You can sit there and learn all about these waves, the high tide and the low tide. The scientists have given us all kinds of explanations but the knowledge about that is not going to be of any help to you. You are not really dealing with anger at all.

Where do you feel the anger, first of all? Where do you feel all these so-called problems you want to be free from "the desires, the burning desires? The desire burns you. Hunger burns you. So the solutions you have or the means of fulfilling them is very simple and makes it impossible for that to burn itself out in your system. Where do you feel the fear? You feel it here in the pit of your stomach. It is part of the body. The body cannot take those high and low tides of energy that are there in your body. So you are wanting to suppress them for some spiritual or social reasons. You are not going to succeed.

Anger is energy, a tremendous outburst of energy, and by destroying that energy, through any means, you are destroying the very expression of life itself. It becomes a problem only when you try to do something with that energy. When it is absorbed by the system you will not do the things that you think you will do if the anger is left alone. You are actually not dealing with the anger but the frustration, or avoiding such a situation which has resulted in clumsiness in your relationships or in your understanding of yourself.

You want to be prepared to meet such situations as and when they arise in the future. The instrument which you are using has been used by you every time there is an outburst of anger yet you have not succeeded in freeing yourself from the anger. You won't come into the possession of anything extraordinary other than this instrument which you have been using all these years, and at the same time you hope that somehow this very thing will help you to be free from the anger tomorrow.

Why are you killing people, thousands of people, for no fault of theirs? Why are you limiting something which is natural but are not condemning the nations that are dropping bombs on helpless people? Do you call them sane? Both of them have sprung from the same source. As long as you do anything to control your anger you will indulge in such atrocious things and justify them because that is the only way to protect your way of life and your way of thinking. These two things go together. Why do you justify that? That is insane. He is not hurting you but he is threatening your way of life. There is a danger of that man taking away what you consider to be your precious things. This idea of stopping this man from acting when there is an outburst of anger is exactly the same. The religious man has found that an angry man will be an antisocial man.

As long as he practices virtue, so long he will remain an antisocial man and he will act out of anger. When that goal that the society has placed before you, when that same goal which you adopted for yourself as an ideal goal to be practiced, is finished for you, you will not harm anybody, either individually or collectively as a nation. You have to deal with the anger. You are dealing with something totally unrelated to the anger. Not even once do you let that anger burn itself out within the framework where it originates and functions. Having some therapy of hitting your pillows, hitting this, that and the other, is just a joke. That does not free the man from the anger once and for all. It will appear again. So what do you do?

You are not dealing with anger. You will never deal with this anger at all as long as you are interested in finding out a way of not hitting the person who is coming with a knife. You have to protect yourself. That is essential. I am not saying for a moment that your anger makes it impossible for you to deal with that situation. Don't say that it's non-violence or you should not hurt somebody else. He is hurting you. Even in the Bible it is an eye for an eye, a tooth for a tooth. You never practice that. Of course, they practice it on a larger scale but in daily life they say it is something terrible to do. I don't see any problem with that at all.

There is no point in discussing hypothetical situations for the simple reason that the person who is hopping mad with anger, burning with anger, will not seek and discuss the question of anger. That's the time to deal with those things, when you are really burning with anger, burning with desire, burning with all those things that you want to be free from. Otherwise, it becomes like a classroom discussion "somebody talking on the anatomy of anger, the anatomy of how the anger arises or the anatomy of love. It's too ridiculous. Or they offer solutions which don't work when there is a real situation. That's the reason why I don't discuss all these things.

No problem, there's no problem for the individual. When he's mad with anger, that's the time for him to deal with it. It stops the thinking. There is no way of separating yourself from the problem. That's what you are trying to do. That is what I mean by saying that you are putting anger out there and trying to look and deal with it as if it is an object outside of you. When you separate yourself, the only result is exactly what you fear would happen. That is inevitable. So you have no way of controlling that at all. Is there anything that you can do to prevent this separation from what you are? It is a horrible thing to realize that you are yourself anger and whatever you do to stop that, prevent it or do something about it is false. That will be tomorrow or in your next life, not now. So that is what you are.

You are not a spiritual man or a religious man. You can imagine that you are a religious man because you are trying to control your anger, or trying to be free from anger, or trying to be less and less angry as the years go by. All that makes you feel that you are not that vicious man whom you avoid. You are no different. You are not any more spiritual than the people whom you condemn. Tomorrow you are going to be a marvelous person. You will be free from anger.

What do you want me to do in the meantime, admire you? Because you have put on the label that you are a spiritual man or you have put on fancy robes? What do you want me to do? For that you want me to admire you? There is nothing there to be admired because you are as vicious as anybody else in this world. Condemning that has no meaning. Adopting a posture which is totally unrelated to what is happening there has no meaning either.

The religious has no meaning when you are pushed into a corner. Then you will behave exactly like anybody else. So this culture "your values, religious or otherwise" haven't touched a bit there. If man is freed from this moral dilemma which has been the basis of the whole thinking of man then he will live like a human being, not a spiritual man, not a religious man. A religious man is no good for the society. A kind man is a menace to the society, one who is practicing kindness as a fine art. All the destruction has come out of them, one who talks of love and one who talks about non-violence. All the destructive forces originated in the thinking of that man.

We are all the inheritors of that culture. We cannot do anything but that. You are freed from the burden of this, the falseness of the whole culture, that's all that I am saying. Individually, you are freed from the totality of all the absurdities that have been imposed upon us. So we are here. We are the inheritors of all that violent culture. Our culture is nothing but to teach man how to kill and how to be killed, whether it is in the name of religion, or in the name of political ideology, or in the name of patriotism, or anything you want. I can't be anything different. That is why I said that the whole thing is moving in the direction of the total annihilation of man. Such things have set in motion forces of destruction which no power can stop.

No power, no god, can stop it because those gods themselves have set in motion these forces of destruction. You see that now happening. When the cave man used the jawbone of an ass to kill his neighbor there were chances of survival for others.

The same cave man who lives there in the White House will set in motion, will let loose forces of destruction, that may completely wipe out every form of life on this planet. It has all come out of that thinking of the man who taught religion, who wanted to establish love on the face of this earth. And see what has been made out of it!

You can stop it in you. Free yourself from that social structure that is operating in you without becoming antisocial, without becoming a reformer, without becoming anti-this, anti-that. You can throw the whole thing out of your system and free yourself from the burden of this culture, for yourself and by yourself. Whether it has any usefulness for society or not is not your concern. If there is one individual who walks free you don't have any more the choking feeling of what this horrible culture has done to you. It's neither East nor West. It's all the same. Human nature is exactly the same. There's no difference.

You are only interested in what to do. How can we stop? Individually, there isn't a damn thing that you can do. When that is understood what is there expresses itself. The intelligence that is there can function much more effectively than all the solutions that man has come out with through his thinking which is the result of millions of years. The ideal that we have placed before us, the perfect man, is just a myth. Such a man doesn't exist at all. The ideal man doesn't exist. It is just a word, an idea. All your life you are trying to become that ideal man and what you are left with is misery, suffering and hope.

Culture has put the demand in you that is pushing you in the direction of wanting to change yourself into something. That is what the culture has done. If you want to do something, Boy, look here, watch your step. That is what they are doing. The second movement that comes, that is the society, Watch your step, it says. So that has put fear in you. Then at the same time it talks of freeing yourself from fear and courage. That is only for the purpose of using you as a pawn in maintaining the status quo of society.

That is why it is teaching courage, it is teaching fearlessness, so that it can use you to maintain the continuity of the society. You are a part of that. That is why every time you want to act what is there is fear and the impossibility of acting.

The society is not out there, the culture is not out there, and unless you are free from that you cannot act. Man is not able to act because he is all the time thinking in terms of the freedom to act. How can I be free to act? That's all that you are concerned about, the freedom. But you are not acting that freedom. The demand for the freedom to act is preventing the action, which is neither social nor antisocial.

You want to bring about a change in yourself. The change is the demand of the society so that you can become a part of that and maintain the continuity of the social structure. When the demand for bringing about any change in you ceases then the concern to change the world around you also comes to an end, ipso facto. You are living in a world of your own. You have created a world of your own experiences and you are trying to project it onto the world. You have no way of experiencing the reality of the world at all. We have to accept all these things as valid because they are workable. They help us to function in this world, to communicate intelligently on that level.

What I am suggesting is that there is no such thing as spirituality at all. If you superimpose what you call spirituality on what is called material life then you create problems for yourself. Because you see growth and development in the material world around you, you are applying that to this so-called spiritual life also. There is only one life. This is a material life and that other has no relevance. Wanting to change your material life into that so-called religious pattern given to you, placed before you by these religious people, is destroying the possibility of your living in harmony and accepting the reality of this material world exactly the way it is. That is responsible for your pain, for your suffering, for your sorrow. It is a constant struggle on your part to be like that and to chase something that does not exist and that has no meaning at all. That gives you the feeling that doing is all that is important for you, not the actual achievement of that. You are moving farther and farther away. The more effort you put into it the more you feel good.

3. 1983-1984: Amsterdam

You are affected by nothing, having erected an impenetrable armor around yourself. You feel nothing. Unable to understand your situation, you react through thought, which is your ideas and mentations. Reaction is thought. The pain you are going through there is clearly reflected without having to experience the pain here. Here there is no experience at all, that is all. In this natural state you feel the pain of others whether you personally know them or not.

Suffering is an experience and there is no experience here. You are not one thing and life another. It is one unitary movement and anything I say about it is misleading, confusing. You are not a person, not a thing, not a discrete entity surrounded by other things. The unitary movement is not something which you can experience.

What I am saying conflicts with your logical framework. You are using logic to continue that separative structure, that is all. Your questions are again thoughts and therefore reactive. All thought is reactive. You are desperately protecting this armor, this shield of thought, and are frightened that the movement of life might smash your frontiers. Life is like a river in spate lashing at the banks, threatening the limits that have been placed around it.

Your thought structure and your actual physiological framework are limited but life itself is not. That is why life in freedom is painful to the body. The tremendous outburst of energy that takes place here is a painful thing to the body, blasting every cell as it goes. You cannot imagine how it is in your wildest dreams. This is why it is misleading no matter how I put it.

Your belief in a unitary movement of life is just a groundless belief, lacking any certainty. You have cleverly rationalized what the gurus and holy books have taught you. Your beliefs are the result of blind acceptance of authority, all secondhand stuff. You are not separate from your beliefs. When your precious beliefs and illusions come to an end, you come to an end. My talking is nothing more than the response to your pain which you are expressing through questions, logical arguments and other mentations. There is nobody here talking, giving advice, feeling pain, or experiencing anything at all. I have nothing here of my own, no obvious or hidden agenda, no product to sell, no axe to grind, nothing to prove.

* * * * *

The body is not concerned with the afterlife or any kind of permanency. It struggles to survive and multiply now. The fictitious beyond, created by thought out of fear, is really the demand for more of the same in modified form. This demand for repetition of the same thing over and over again is the demand for permanence. Such permanence is foreign to the body. Thought's demand for permanence is choking the body and distorting perception. Thought sees itself as not just the protector of its own continuity but also of the body's continuity. Both are utterly false.

You will continue doing what you are doing. Its meaninglessness does not even occur to you. I tell you, when you stop doing things out of hope and the desire for continuity, all you do along with it stops. You will stay afloat. But still the hope remains there, There must be some way, perhaps I am not doing it the right way. In other words, we have to accept the absurdity of depending upon anything. We must face our helplessness.

Your problems continue because of the false solutions you have invented. If the answers are not there the questions cannot be there. They are interdependent. Your problems and solutions go together. Because you want to use certain answers to end your problems, those problems continue. The numerous solutions offered by all these holy people "the psychologists, the politicians" are not really solutions at all. That is obvious. If there were legitimate answers there would be no problems. They can only exhort you to try harder, practice more meditations, love, and more and more of the same. That is all they can do.

The teacher, guru or leader who offers solutions is also false, along with his so-called answers. He is not doing any honest work, only selling a cheap, shoddy commodity in the marketplace. If you brushed aside your hope, fear and naivetÃ©, and treated these fellows like businessmen, you would see that they do not deliver the goods and never will. But you go on and on buying these bogus wares offered up by the experts.

All their philosophies cannot compare to the native wisdom of the body itself. What they are calling mental activity, spiritual activity, emotional activity and feelings are really all one unitary process. This body is highly intelligent and does not need these scientific or theological teachings to survive and procreate. Take away all your fancies about life, death and freedom, and the body remains unscathed, functioning harmoniously. It does not need your or my help. You don't have to do a thing.

* * * * *

The body knows that it will come to an end in that particular form only to continue on in others. Those leaders who would direct your spiritual life cannot be honest about these things for they make a living out of fear, speculations about future life and the mystery of death. And as for you, the followers, you are not really interested in the future of man, only in your own petty little destinies.

You are all neurotic people. You talk against birth control, drone on and on about the preciousness of life, then bomb and massacre. It is too absurd. You are concerned with an unborn life while you are killing thousands and thousands of people by bombing, starvation, poverty and terrorism. Your concern about life is only to make a political issue out of it. It is just an academic discussion.

Are you interested in the future of mankind? Your expressions of anger, righteousness and caring have no meaning to me. It is just a ritual. You sit and talk, that's all. You are not at all angry. If you were angry at this moment you would not ask this question even to yourself. You sit everlastingly talking of anger. The angry wouldn't talk about it. The body has already acted with regard to that anger by absorbing it. The anger is burnt, finished then and there. You don't do anything. The body just absorbs it, that is all. If all this is too much for you, if it depresses you, don't ever go to the holy men. Do anything but don't expect the holy business to help you. It is a waste of time.

All moral, spiritual, ethical values are false. The psychologists, searching for a pragmatic way out, are now at the end of their tethers, even turning to the spiritual people for answers. They are lost and yet the answers must come from them, not from the encrusted, useless traditions of the holy business.

The so-called messiahs have left nothing but misery in this world. If a modern messiah came before you, he would be unable to help you at all. And if he can't help no one can. Truth is a movement. You can't capture it, contain it, give expression to it or use it to advance your interests. The moment you capture it, it ceases to be the truth. What is the truth for me is something that cannot, under any circumstances, be communicated to you.

The certainty here cannot be transmitted to another. For this reason, the whole guru business is absolute nonsense. This has always been the case, not just now. Your self-denial is to enrich the priests. Those in the holy business thrive on the stupidity and credulity of others. The politicians, similarly, thrive on the gullibility of man. It is the same everywhere.

When you die, the body is in a prostrate position. It stops functioning and that is the end of it. But in this case, the body somehow renewed itself. It happens daily as a matter of course now. The whole process took years to stabilize. For me, life and death are one, not two separate things. Just let me warn you that if what you are aiming at, enlightenment, really happens you will die. There will be a physical death because there has to be a physical death to be in that state. It is like playing around with controlling your breath because you find it amusing. But if you hold the breath long enough you choke to death.

To describe that state as a meditative state full of awareness is romantic hogwash. Awareness "what a fantastic gimmick used to fool themselves and others. You can't be aware of every step. You only become self-conscious and awkward if you try. I once knew a man who was a harbor pilot. He had been reading about passive awareness and attempted to put it into practice. For the first time he nearly wrecked the ship he was guiding. Walking is automatic and if you try to be aware of every step you will go crazy. So don't invent meditative steps. Things are bad enough. The meditative state is worse.

Any remedy I offered you would become part of your search, that is, more romantic stuff. That is why I never tire of saying that I have no wares to sell, much less offer you new and better methods, whereby you can continue your search. I deny the validity of that search entirely.

If your meditations, methods and techniques meant anything you wouldn't be here asking these questions. They are all means for you to bring about change. I maintain that there is nothing to change or transform. You accept that there is something to change as an article of faith. You never question the existence of the one who is to be changed. The whole mystique of enlightenment is based upon the idea of transforming yourself. I cannot convey or transmit my certainty that you, and all the authorities down through the centuries, are false. They, and the spiritual goods they peddle, are utterly false.

* * * * *

There is no particular charm in being antisocial. I don't give people what they want. When they realize they will not get what they want here they invariably go away. As they are leaving for the last time I like to add the rider, You won't get it anywhere. When people come to talk they find themselves confronted with silence itself. That is why everybody who comes is automatically silent thereafter. If he cannot stand the silence and insists upon talking and discussing things he will be forced to disagree and walk out.

But if you stay long you will be silenced, not because it is over-persuasive, more rational than you are, but because it is silence itself silencing that movement there. That silence burns everything here. All experiences are burnt. That is why talking to people doesn't exhaust me. It is energy to me. That is why I can talk for the whole day without showing any fatigue. Talking with so many people over the years has had no impact upon me. All that I or they have said is burnt here, leaving no trace. This is not, unfortunately, the case with you.

* * * * *

Any action that takes place at the conscious level of your thinking existence is a reaction. The one and only action is the response of this living organism to the stimuli around it. That stimulus-response process is a unitary phenomenon. There is no division between action and reaction except when thought interferes and artificially separates them. Otherwise, it is an automatic, unitary process and there is nothing you can do to stop it.

Just as in reality there is no separation of action and reaction, so there is no room for the religious man in the natural scheme of things. The fresh movement of life threatens his source of power and prestige. Still, he does not want to retire. He must be thrown out. Religion is not a contractual arrangement, either public or private. It has nothing to do with the social structure or its management. Religious authority wants to continue its hold on the people but religion is entirely an individual affair.

I am simply pointing out the absurdity of this conversation. Once you get the hang of it you just go. I have no message to give mankind.

* * * * *

We have set in motion irreversible forces. We have polluted the sky, the waters, everything. Only technology progresses, while we as a race are moving closer to complete and total destruction of ourselves and the world. Everything in man's consciousness is pushing the whole world, which nature has so laboriously created, towards destruction. There has been no qualitative change in man's thinking. We feel about our neighbors just as the frightened cave man felt towards his. The only thing that has changed is our ability to destroy our neighbor and his property.

Violence is an integral part of the evolutionary process. That violence is essential for the survival of the living organism. You can't condemn the hydrogen bomb for it is an extension of the policeman there and your desire to be protected. Where do you draw the line? You can't. We have no way of reversing the whole thing.

* * * * *

Love and hate are the same. They have together resulted in massacre, murder, assassination and wars. This is a matter of history, not my opinion. It is the same thing everywhere. All our political systems have come out of that religious thinking, whether of the East or of the West. In light of these facts, how can you have any faith in religion? What is the good of reviving the whole past, the useless past? It is because your living has no meaning to you that you dwell on the past. You are not even drifting. You have no direction at all. You are just floating. Obviously, there is no purpose to your life, otherwise you would not live in the past.

What has not helped you cannot help anybody. No matter what I am saying, you are the medium of expression. You have already captured what I am saying and are making of it a new ideology and means to attain something. What I am trying to say is that you must discover something for yourself. But do not be misled into thinking that what you find will be of use to society, that it can be used to change the world. You are finished with society, that is all.

* * * * *

God is the ultimate pleasure, uninterrupted happiness. No such thing exists. Your wanting something that does not exist is the root of your problem. Transformation, liberation and all that stuff are just variations on the same theme, permanent happiness. The body cannot take that. The pleasure of sex, for instance, is by nature temporary. The body can't take uninterrupted pleasure for long. It would be destroyed. Wanting to impose a fictitious, permanent state of happiness on the body is a serious neurological problem. It never strikes you that the enlightenment and God you are after is just the ultimate pleasure, a pleasure, moreover, which you have invented.

* * * * *

If I narrate the story of my life it is as if I am describing somebody else's life. There is no attachment, sentiment or emotional content for me when I consider my life. You get the wrong impression if you think I harbor any private, precious thoughts or feelings regarding my past.

What is the difference whether or not you find this freedom, this enlightenment, or not? You will not be there to benefit from it. What possible good can this state do you? This state takes away everything you have. While living, the body has died. Somehow, the body, having gone through death, is kept alive. Here you lose everything.

I am only saying that you must go find out for yourself if there is anything behind these meaningless abstractions being thrown at you, all the abstract, mystical terms used to seduce gullible people. Life has to be described in pure and simple physical and physiological terms. It must be demystified and depsychologized.

Don't talk of higher centers and chakras. It is not these but glands that control the human body. It is the glands that give the instructions for the functioning of this organism. In your case, you have introduced an interloper, thought. In your natural state, thought ceases to control anything. It comes into temporary function when a challenge is put before it, immediately falling into the background when it is no longer needed.

Forget about the ideal society and the ideal human being. Just look at the way you are functioning, that is the important thing. What has prevented the organism from fully flowering into its own uniqueness is culture. It has placed the wrong thing, the ideal person, before man. The whole thing is born out of the divisive consciousness of mankind. It has brought us nothing but violence. That is why no two gurus or saviors ever agree. Each is intent upon preaching his own nonsense.

You want to know. You believe that in knowing my story you will be able to duplicate what happened to me. You, having been brainwashed all your life, can only think in terms of imitation. You think that somehow you can repeat what happened to me, that is all. That is your motive for coming.

It is not a new approach to that religious stuff. It is completely different. It has absolutely nothing to do with all that romantic, spiritual, religious stuff. If you translate what I am saying into religious terms you are missing the point entirely. Religion, God, soul, are all just words, ideas used to keep your psychological continuity intact. When these thoughts are not there, what is left is the simple, harmonious physical functioning of the organism.

I am able to describe the way this organism is functioning because your question has created the challenge here. Your questions create the conditions necessary for this response to happen. So it is describing itself, but that is not the way it is functioning. It functions in a state of not knowing. I never ask myself how I am functioning. I never question my actions before, during or after they occur. You can't fit me into a category. Any attempt on your part to translate what I am saying into your religious framework is to miss the point. I am not one of your holy men who say, "I am hanging so come hang with me." All that stuff is a form of madness.

Your intellectual understanding, in which you have a tremendous investment, has not done one damn thing for you so far. You persist in the cultivation of this intellectual understanding knowing all the while that it has never helped you at all. This is amazing. When hoping and attempting to understand is not there then life becomes meaningful.

Life, your existence, has a tremendous living quality about it. All your notions about love, infinite bliss and peace only block this natural energy of existence. How can I make you understand that what I am describing has absolutely nothing to do with all that religious stuff? It is really something. It is no good throwing all this junk at me. Whatever hits this is immediately burnt. That is the nature of the energy here.

The spiritual people are the most dishonest people. I am emphasizing that foundation upon which the whole of spirituality is built. If there is no spirit then the whole talk of spirituality is bosh and nonsense. You can't come into your own being until you are free from the whole thing surrounding the concept of self. To be really on your own, the whole basis of spiritual life, which is erroneous, has to be destroyed. It does not mean that you become fanatical or violent, burning down temples, tearing down the idols, destroying the holy books like a bunch of drunks. It is not that at all. It is a bonfire inside of you. Everything that mankind has thought and experienced must go. The incredible violence in the world today has been created by the Jesuses and Buddhas.

It is the ones who believe in God, who preach peace and talk of love, who have created the human jungle. Compared to man's jungle, nature's jungle is simple and sensible! The so-called civilized man kills for ideals and beliefs while the animals kill only for survival. Because man is worse than other animals it made it necessary and possible for him to create the moral dilemma. When man first experienced the division in his consciousness, when he experienced his self-consciousness, he felt superior to other animals, which he is not, and therein sowed the seeds of his own destruction.

* * * * *

Awareness is not a divided state. There are not two states, awareness and something else. There are not two things. It is not that you are aware of something. Awareness is simply the action of the brain. The idea that you can use awareness to bring about some happier state of affairs, some sort of transformation or God-knows-what, is absurd. Awareness cannot be used to bring about a change in yourself or the world around you.

All this rubbish about the conscious and the unconscious, awareness and the self, is all a product of modern psychology. The idea that you can use awareness to get somewhere psychologically is very damaging. After more than a hundred years we seem unable to free ourselves from the psychological rubbish, Freud and the whole gang.

Just what exactly do you mean by consciousness? You are conscious, aware, only through thought. The other animals use thought. The dog, for example, can recognize its owner in a simple manner. They recognize without using language. Humans have added to the structure of thought, making it much more complex.

Thought is not yours or mine. It is our common inheritance. There is no such thing as your mind and my mind. There is only mind, the totality of all that has been known, felt and experienced by man, handed down from generation to generation. We are all thinking and functioning in that thought sphere just as we all share the same atmosphere for breathing. The thoughts are there to function and communicate in this world sanely and intelligently.

Knowledge "that is all that is there. The self is nothing more than the totality of the inherited knowledge passed on to us from generation to generation. You teach the child to distinguish between colors, to read, to imitate manners. It is relative to each culture. Gestures and expressions constituted the first language. Later, words were added on. We still use gestures to supplement our spoken words because we feel that words alone are inadequate to fully express what we want to convey.

All this is not to say that we can really know anything about thought. We can't. You become conscious of thought only when you make it an object of thought. Otherwise, you don't even know you are thinking. We use thought only to understand something out there, to remember something or to achieve something. Otherwise, we don't even know if thought is there or not. Thought is not separate from the movement of thought. Thought is action and without it you cannot act. There is no such thing as pure, spontaneous, thought-free action at all. To act is to think.

You have a self-starting, self-perpetuating mechanism which I call the self. This does not mean that there is actually an entity there. I do not want or mean to give that connotation to that word. Where is this ego or self that you talk of? Your non-existent self has heard of spirituality and bliss from someone. To experience this thing called bliss you feel you must control your thoughts. It is impossible. You will burn yourself and die if you attempt it.

The demand for more and more experience constitutes your present, which is born out of the past. If that is seen, there is no future at all. Any achievement you are interested in is in the future. The only way that the future can come into operation is in the present moment. Unfortunately, in the present moment what is in operation is the past. Your past is creating your future. In the past you were happy or unhappy, foolish or wise. In the future you will be the opposite.

When the past is not in operation there is no present at all, for what you are calling the present is the past repeating itself. In an actual state of here and now there is no past in operation and therefore no future. The only way the past can survive and maintain its continuity is through the constant demand to experience the same thing over and over. That is why life has become a bore. Life has become boring because we have made of it a repetitive thing. So what we mistakenly call the present is really the repetitive past projecting a fictitious future. Your goals, your search, your aspirations, are cast in that mold.

From your knowledge out of the past you ask questions and the very motive of your asking is only to gain more knowledge from someone else so that your knowledge structure can continue. You are really not interested in this at all. Your knowledge coming to an end means that you are coming to an end. Where, you ask, is this knowledge, the past? Is it in your brain? Where is it? It is all over your body. It is in every cell of your body.

It doesn't matter what the object of that search is "God, a beautiful woman, whatsoever" it is all the same search and that hunger will never be satisfied. That hunger must burn itself out completely without knowing satisfaction. The thirst you have must burn itself out without being quenched. It dawns on you that this is not the way and it is finished.

What I am emphasizing is that we are trying to solve our basic human problems through a psychological framework when actually the problem is neurological. The body is involved. Take desire. As long as there is a living body, there will be desire. It is natural. Thought has interfered and tried to suppress, control and moralize about desire to the detriment of mankind. We are trying to solve the problem of desire through thought. It is thinking that has created the problem. You somehow continue to hope and believe that the same instrument can solve your other problems as well. You hope against hope that thought will pull you through but you will die in hope just as you have lived in hope. That is the refrain of my doom song.

* * * * *

Unless you are free from the desire of all desires "liberation or self-realization" you will be miserable. The ultimate goal which society has placed before us is the one that has to go. Until you are free from that desire you cannot be free from any of your miseries. By suppressing these desires you are not going to be free. This realization is the essential thing, going as it does to the crux of the problem.

It is society that has placed before us the desire for freedom, the desire for liberation, the desire for God, the desire for self-realization. That is the desire you must be free from. Then all these other desires fall into their own natural rhythm. You suppress these desires only because you are afraid society will punish you if you act on them or because you see them as obstacles to your main desire, freedom.

If this kind of thing should happen to you, you will find yourself back in a primeval state, without primitivity and without any volition on your part. It just happens. Such a free man is not in conflict with society any more. He is not antisocial, not at war with the world. He sees that it can't be any the different. He doesn't want to change society at all. The demand for change has ceased. Any doing in any direction is violence. Any effort is violence. Anything you do with thought to create a peaceful state of mind is using force and so is violent. Such an approach is absurd. You are trying to enforce peace through violence. Meditation is violent. The living organism is very peaceful. You don't have to do a thing. The peacefully functioning body doesn't give a damn for your ecstasies or blissful states. People have abandoned the natural intelligence of the body.

All I am saying is that the peace you are seeking is already inside you in the harmonious functioning of the body. Anything you do to free yourself from anything, for whatever reason, is destroying the sensitivity, clarity and freedom that is already there.

* * * * *

There is no question of your seeing things as they are. You can't see things as they are. You never leave any experience or feeling you have alone. You have to capture and interpret that feeling within the framework of the known. You are happy or unhappy only as you have knowledge about and experience of happiness and unhappiness. So everything has to be brought within the framework of the known before you can experience it. The movement of the known is gathering momentum within you. Its only interest is to continue. There is no entity, nothing there to give itself continuity. It is just the movement of thought, the self-perpetuating separation. It is mechanical. Anything you try to do about it only adds momentum to it.

It is the desire to reach a particular goal, an all important goal, that must go, not the countless petty little desires. The only reason you try to manipulate or control the petty desires is that such control is a part of your strategy to attain the highest goal, the desire of all desires. Eliminate that main goal and the others fall into a natural pattern and pose no problem for you or for the world. You won't get anywhere by trying to endlessly control and manipulate these numerous desires. It is vicious in its nature.

The so-called highest goal is like the horizon. The further you move towards it the further it recedes. The goal, like the horizon, is not really there. It is a projection of your own fear and it moves away from you as you pursue it. How can you keep up with it? There is nothing that you can do. Still, it is desire that keeps you moving. No matter in which direction you move, it is the same.

What you experience through your separative consciousness is an illusion. You can't say that falling bombs are an illusion. It is not an illusion. Only your experience of it is an illusion. The reality of the world that you are experiencing now is an illusion. That is all I am trying to say.

* * * * *

There is no such thing as absolute. It is thought and thought alone that has created the absolute. Absolute zero, absolute power, absolute perfection, these have been invented by the holy men and experts. They kidded themselves and others. Down the centuries, the saints, saviors and prophets of mankind have kidded themselves and everybody else. Perfection and absolutes are false. You are trying to imitate and relate your behavior according to these absolutes and it is falsifying you. You are actually functioning in an entirely different way. You are brutal. You feel you must be peaceful. It is contradictory. That's all I'm pointing out.

* * * * *

The certainty that dawned upon me is something which cannot be transmitted. It does not mean that I am superior, a chosen one, one in whom all the virtues are rolled into one, not at all. I am just an ordinary man and have nothing to do with it. This certainly blasts everything including the claims of the so-called religious.

What I am trying to put across is that there is no such thing as God. It is the mind that out of fear has created God. Fear is passed on from generation to generation. What is there is fear, not God. If you are lucky enough to be free from fear then there is no God. There is no ultimate reality, no God, nothing. Fear itself is the problem, not God. Wanting to be free from fear is itself fear. You see, you love fear. The ending of fear is death and you don't want that to happen. I am not talking of wiping out the phobias of the body. They are necessary for survival. The death of fear is the only death.

* * * * *

You are blind. You see nothing. When you actually do see and perceive for the first time that there is no self to realize, no psyche to purify, no soul to liberate, it will come as a tremendous shock to that instrument. You have invested everything in that "the soul, mind, psyche, what-ever you wish to call it" and suddenly it is exploded as a myth. It is difficult for you to look at reality, at your actual situation. One look does the trick. You are finished.

I don't see anything other than the physical activity of the body. Spirituality is the invention of the mind and the mind is a myth. Your traditions are choking you but, unfortunately, you don't do anything. You actually love being choked. You love the burden of the cultural garbage sack, the dead refuse of the past. It has to drop away naturally. It just drops. You don't depend upon knowledge anymore except as a useful tool to function sanely in this world.

Wanting has to go. Wanting to be free from something that is not there is what you call sorrow. Sorrow is there for you as long as you think. There is actually no sorrow there to be free from. Thinking about and struggling against sorrow is sorrow. Since you can't stop thinking, and thinking is sorrow, you will always suffer. There is no way out, no escape.

Suppose I say that this meaninglessness is all there is for you, all there can ever be for you. What will you do? The false and absurd goal you have before you is responsible for that dis-satisfaction and meaninglessness in you. Do you think life has any meaning? Obviously, you don't. You have been told that there is meaning, that there must be a meaning to life. Your notion of the meaningful keeps you from facing this issue and makes you feel that life has no meaning. If the idea of the meaningful is dropped then you will see meaning in whatever you are doing in daily life.

Whatever you want, even the so-called spiritual goals, is materialistic in value. What, if I may ask, is so spiritual about it? If you want to achieve a spiritual goal, the instrument you use will be the same which you use to achieve materialistic goals, namely thought. You don't actually do anything about it. You just think. So you are just thinking that there must be some purpose to life. And because thought is matter, its object, the spiritual or meaningful life, is also matter. Spirituality is materialism. In any event, you do not act, you just think, which is to postpone. There is simply nothing else thought can do.

That instrument called thought, which you are employing to achieve your so-called spiritual goals, is the result of the past. Thought is born in time, it functions in time and any results it seeks are bound to be in and of time also. And time is postponement, the tomorrow.

Understanding your goal is the main thing. To achieve that goal implies struggle, battle, effort, will, that is all. There is no guarantee that you will reach your goal. You assume the goal is there. You have invented the goal to give yourself hope but hope means tomorrow. Hope is necessary for tomorrow, not for today. You want more knowledge so you can develop better techniques for reaching your goal. You know that there is no guarantee that more experience, more knowledge, more systems and more methods will help you reach your goal yet you persist. It is all you know how to do. Seeing today demands action. Seeing tomorrow involves only hope.

The energy you are devoting to the search, or whatever you wish to call it, is taking away the energy you need to live. You are obsessed with finding meaning in life and that is consuming a lot of energy. If that energy is released from the search for meaning it can be used to see the futility of all search. Then your life becomes meaningful and the energy may be used for some useful purpose. Life, the so-called material life, has a meaning of its own, but you have been told that it is devoid of meaning and have superimposed a fictitious layer of spiritual meaning over it.

There is nothing to be achieved, nothing to accomplish. Here there is no need to sit in special postures and control your breath. Even while my eyes are open, in fact no matter what I am doing, I am in a state of moksha. The knowledge you have about moksha is what is keeping you away from it. Moksha comes after the ending of all you have ever known, at death. The body has to become like a corpse before that knowledge, which is locked into every cell in the body, ceases.

* * * * *

Your highly praised inventiveness springs from your thinking, which is essentially a protective mechanism. The mind has invented both religion and dynamite to protect what it regards as its best interests. There is no good or bad in this sense. Don't you see? All these bad, brutal, terrible people who should have been eliminated long ago are thriving and successful. Don't think that you can get off this merry-go-round or that by pretending to be spiritually superior you are avoiding any complicity. You are that.

* * * * *

There is no love in the world. Everybody wants the same thing. Whosoever is the most ruthless gets it, as long as he can get away with it. Getting what you want in this world is a relatively easy thing if you are ruthless enough. I had everything a man could want, every kind of desirable experience, and it all failed me. Therefore, I can never recommend my path to anyone, having eventually faced the falseness of that path myself and rejected it. I would never even hint that there was any validity in all those experiences and practices.

* * * * *

The prophets were all wrong, as far as I am concerned. As long as you harbor any hope or faith in these authorities, living or dead, so long this certainty cannot be transmitted to you. This certainty somehow dawns on you when you see for yourself that all of them are wrong. When you see all this for yourself for the first time you explode. That explosion hits life at a point that has never been touched before. It is absolutely unique.

So whatever I may be saying cannot be true for you. The moment you see it for yourself, you make what I am saying obsolete and false. All that came before is negated in that fire. You can't come into your own uniqueness unless the whole of human experience is thrown out of your system. It cannot be done through any volition or the help of anything. Then you are on your own.

* * * * *

When once you are freed from the pairs of opposites "right and wrong, good and bad" you will never be wrong. But until then the problem will be there. It is like accidentally touching a live wire. You are much too frightened to touch it through your own volition. By sheer accident, this thing touches you, burning everything. It burns out this search, the hunger. The hunger stops, not because it is satisfied. The hunger can never be satiated, especially by the traditional food that is offered. With the burning away of that hunger the duality ceases, that is all.

* * * * *

My interest is not to knock off what others have said (that is too easy) but to knock off what I am saying. More precisely, I am trying to stop what you are making out of what I am saying. This is why my talking sounds contradictory to others. I am forced by the nature of your listening to always negate the first statement with another statement. Then the second statement is negated by a third and so on. My aim is not some comfy dialectical thesis but the total negation of everything that can be expressed.

Anything you try to make out of my statements is not it. You sense a freshness, a living quality, to what is being said here. That is so, but this cannot be used for anything. It is worthless. All you can do with it is to try to organize it, create organizations, open schools, publish holy books, celebrate birthdays, sanctify holy temples and the like, thus destroying any life it may have had in it. No individual can be helped by such things. They only help those who would live by the gullibility of others.

* * * * *

There was an outburst of energy which is utterly different from the energy that is born out of thinking. All spiritual, mystical experiences are born out of thought. They are thought-induced states, nothing more. The energy here that is burning all thought as it arises tends to accumulate, eventually it has to escape. The physical limitations of the body act as obstacles to the escape of this unique energy. When it escapes it goes up, never down, and never returns.

When this extraordinary energy, which is atomic, escapes it causes tremendous pain. It is not the pain you are familiar with. It has nothing to do with it. If it did, the body would be shattered. It is not matter converting into energy. It is atomic. The process goes on and on while the pain comes and goes. It is like the tremendous relief when a tooth is extracted. That is the kind of relief that is there, not the spiritual.

The translation of this as bliss is very misleading. Through thought anyone can create those experiences but it is not actually bliss. The real thing is not something that can be experienced. Anything you can experience is old. That means everything you experience or understand is tradition.

In other words, I am trying to free you not from the past, the conditioning, but rather from what I am saying. I am not suggesting any way out because there is no way. I have stumbled

70

into this and freed myself from the paths of others. I can't make the same mistake they did. I will never suggest that anyone use me as a model or follow in my footsteps.

My path can never be your path. If you attempt to make this your path you will get caught in a rut. No matter how refreshing, revolutionary or fantastic, it is still a rut, a copy, a secondhand thing. I myself do not know how I stumbled into this so how do you expect me to give it to another? My mission, if there is any, is to debunk every statement I have ever made. If you take seriously and try to use or apply what I have said you will be in danger.

Moksha cannot be transmitted to another because there is nothing there to transmit. Neither is there anything to renounce. What is it that these teachers suggest you should renounce? Even your scripture, the Kathopanishad, says that you must renounce the very search itself. The renunciation of renunciation happens not through practice, discussion, money or intellect. These are the least of things. A rough translation of the original Sanskrit is, Whomsoever it chooses, to him it is revealed. If this is so then where is the room for practices and volition? It comes randomly, not because you deserve it.

If you are lucky enough to have this dawn on you, you die. The continuity of thought dies. The ending of thought is the beginning of physical death. What you experience is the emptiness of the void. Just wanting to be free of egoism is insufficient. You must go through a clinical death to be free from thought and egoism. The body will actually get stiff, the heartbeat slows and you will become corpse-like. The ideas you have about that natural state are totally unrelated to what it actually is. You are trying to capture and give expression to what you hope is that state. It is an absurd exercise. What is there is only the movement to capture, nothing else. All the rest is speculation.

* * * * *

Knowledge is not something mysterious or abstract. Knowledge is just naming things. The knowledge you have of the world creates the objects you are experiencing. The actual existence or non-existence of something out there in the world is not something you can determine or experience for yourself except through the help of knowledge, and this knowledge is not yours. It is something which you and your ancestors have accumulated over a long time. What you call the act of knowing is nothing other than this accumulated memory. You have personally added to and modified that knowledge but essentially it doesn't belong to you at all.

There is nothing there inside you but the totality of this knowledge you have accumulated. That is what you are. You cannot even directly experience the reality of the world in which you are functioning, much less some world beyond. There is no world beyond space and time. It is your invention based upon the vague promises of the holy men. Our sense of value springs from the world as it is imposed on us. We must accept the world.

Tradition is what you are, what you call you. No matter how you may modify it, it continues. In life, everything is temporary, and the attempt to give continuity to conditioning, which is based upon thought, is pathological in nature. You treat the psychological and the pathological as if they were two different things. Actually, there is only the pathological there. Your conditioning that makes you feel separate from yourself and the world is pathological.

All your actions spring from the same source, thinking. The thoughts themselves cannot do any harm. It is when you attempt to use, censor and control those thoughts to get something that your problems begin. You have no recourse but to use thought to get what you want in this world, but when you seek to get what does not exist "God, bliss, love, etc." through thought you only succeed in pitting one thought against another, creating misery for yourself and the world.

When the thought structure, pressed into the service of fear and hope, cannot achieve what it wants, or cannot be certain, it introduces what you call faith. When your beliefs have gotten you nowhere you are told you must cultivate faith. In other words, you must have hope. Whether you are seeking God or bliss, peace of mind or, more tangibly, happiness, you end up relying on hope, belief and faith. These dependencies are the tokens of your failure to get the results you desire.

Every thought that is born has to die. If a thought does not die it cannot be reborn. It has to die and with it you die. But instead of dying with each thought and breath, you hook up each thought with the next, creating a false continuity. It is that continuity that is the problem. Your insecurity springs from your refusal to face the temporary nature of thought. It is a little easier to talk to those who have meditated because they experience the futility of it and can see where they are hung up.

* * * * *

Your morality, or the lack of it, is of no importance compared to the fact that you are dead. You are always operating in and through your dead memory. Memory is nothing more than the same old nonsense repeating itself, that's all. All you know or can ever know is memory, and memory is thought. Your ceaseless thinking is only giving you continuity. Why do you have to do that all the time? It is not worth it. You are wearing yourself out. When there is a need for it one can understand.

You are mulling over the future or the past all the time, oblivious to the present. There is no future in relation to your problem. Any solution you think of is in the future and is therefore useless. If there is anything that can happen it must happen now. Since you don't want anything to happen now you push it away into something you have named the future. What you have in place of the present is fear. Then begins the whole exhausting search for a way to be free from fear. Do you really want this kind of freedom?

Anything you want to be free from, for whatever reason, is the very thing that can free you. You are always dealing with a pair of opposites, so being free of one is to be free from the other, its opposite. Within the framework of the opposites there is no freedom. That is why I always say, You haven't got a chance. Likewise, the man who is not concerned with morality will not be interested in immorality. The answer to selfishness lies in selfishness, not a fictitious opposite called selflessness. Freedom from anger lies in anger, not in non-anger. Freedom from greed lies in greed, not in non-greed.

The whole religious business is nothing but moral codes of conduct. You must be generous, compassionate, loving, while all the time you remain greedy and callous. Codes of conduct are set by society in its own interests, sacred or profane. There is nothing religious about it. The religious man puts the priest, the censor, inside you. Now the policeman has been institutionalized and placed outside you. Religious codes and strictures are no longer necessary. It is all in the civil and criminal codes. You needn't bother with these religious people anymore. They are obsolete. But they don't want to lose their hold over people. It is their business. Their livelihood is at stake.

* * * * *

Your search for happiness only succeeds in destroying the sensitivity and intelligence of the nervous system. Wanting what does not exist "the romantic, religious, spiritual stuff" only adds momentum to that false continuity, which destroys the body. It is radically disturbing the chemical balance of the body. The body, which is only interested in survival and procreation, treats both pain and pleasure alike. It is you who insist on stopping pain and extending pleasure. The body's response to both pleasure and pain is the same, it groans. What does the body want? It doesn't want anything except to function. All other things are the inventions of thought.

The body has no separate, independent existence of its own apart from pleasure and pain. The various vibrations affecting the body may differ in intensity but it is you who divide them into good and bad. You are constantly translating vibrations that hit the body into experiences. The body's natural intelligence is correctly processing the sensory input without your having to do a thing. It is similar to how the body turns over many times during sleep without your being aware of it, much less trying to control it. The body is handling itself.

You are all the time interfering with the natural functioning of the nervous system. When a sensation hits your nervous system, the first thing you do is to name it and categorize it as pleasure or pain. The next step is that you want to continue the pleasurable sensations and stop the painful sensations. First, the recognition of a sensation as pleasure or pain is itself painful. Second, the attempt to extend the life of one kind of sensation and to stop another kind of sensation is also painful.

Both activities are choking the body. In the very nature of things, every sensation has its own intensity and duration. The attempt to extend pleasure and stop pain only succeeds in destroying the sensitivity of the body and its ability to respond to sensations. So what you are doing is very painful for the body.

If you do nothing with the sensations, you will find that they must dissolve into themselves. That is what I mean when I speak of the ionization of thought. That is what I mean by birth and death. There is no death for the body, only disintegration.

Thought being material, all its pursuits are material. That is why your so called spiritual pursuits have no meaning. Don't get me wrong, I am not against using thought to get what you need. You have no other tool at your disposal.

So the body is interested only in its survival. All that are necessary for life are the survival and reproductive systems. That is nature's way. Why life wants to reproduce itself is another matter. The only way the human organism can survive and ensure its reproduction is through thought. So thought is very important and even essential to the living organism. Thought determines whether there is action or no action. All animals have these survival thoughts but in the case of man the factor of recognition is introduced, complicating the whole thing enormously. We have superimposed over the natural sensory functioning a never-ending verbalization.

The body is not at all interested in psychological or spiritual matters. Your highly praised spiritual experiences are of no value to the organism. In fact, they are painful to the body. Love, compassion, understanding, bliss "all these things which religion and psychology have placed before man are only adding to the strain of the body. All cultures, whether of the Orient or of the Occident, have created this lopsided situation for mankind and turned man into a neurotic individual.

Instead of being what you are, unkind, you pursue the fictitious opposite put before you, kindness. To emphasize what we should be only causes strain, giving momentum to what we already in fact are. In nature, we find the animals at one time violent and brutal, at others kind and generous. For them there is no contradiction. But man is told he must be always good, kind, loving. We emphasize only one side of reality thus distorting the whole picture. This trying to have one without the other is creating tremendous strain, sorrow, pain and misery for man.

Actually, you are born and die with every breath you take. That is what is meant by death and rebirth. Your thought structure denies the reality of death. It seeks continuity at all costs. I am only pointing out that if you go deep enough, the you disappears, the body goes through an actual clinical death, and that, in some cases, the body can renew itself. At that point, the entire history of the individual, located in the body's genetic structure, no longer separates itself from life, and falls into its own rhythm. From then on it cannot separate itself from anything. You can no longer create this division in consciousness between waking and sleeping.

So don't bother theorizing about thoughtless states. When thought is finished, you die. Until then, all talk of thoughtless states are the silly products of thought trying to give itself continuity by believing in and searching out a thoughtless state. If you have ever fancied yourself to be in a thoughtless state it means that thought was there.

You need not practice any yogic techniques in order to experience these things. By taking drugs you can have all these experiences. I am not at all advocating drugs any more than I am advocating yoga. I am just pointing out that all experience is born out of thought and is in all the essentials identical. If you call these yogic or drug-induced states blissful, more profound or in any way more pleasurable than ordinary experiences, you are strengthening the ego and fortifying the separative structure by wasting your thoughts, translating sensations into higher or lower and pleasurable or painful. Anything you experience as energy is thought-induced energy. It is not the energy of life.

* * * * *

What are you, essentially? Look, in this state there is no division. Our situation is that I cannot transmit and you cannot receive that fact. In addition to it you have gone one step further and created a more complex problem for yourself by placing the undivided state outside yourself as you are. This means search. To search is willful. The search for peace is dulling the natural peacefulness of the body. Your knowledge and search are meaningless because there is nothing inside the division you have created around you.

It is all worthless as far as you are concerned. It is a menu without the meal. It is all a sales pitch. It has resulted in hypocrisy and commercialism. There is something radically wrong with it. If there is anything good it cannot produce anything bad. Obviously, religions are false "religion, spirituality, society, you, your property, your motives and values, the whole thing.

I am not here to teach you anything. This is not a didactic or instructional exercise. Words only have a vague abstract meaning for you. Otherwise, they have no relevance to you at all. You have to be saved from the very idea that you have to be saved. You must be saved from the saviors, redeemed from the redeemers. If it is to happen it must happen now. My words cannot penetrate the lunacy there. It is the madness of the spiritual search that makes you unmoved and impervious to my words.

Forget the rosaries, the scriptures, the ashes on your forehead. When you see for yourself the absurdity of your search, the whole culture is reduced to ashes inside you. Then you are out of that. Tradition is finished for you. No more games. Vedanta means the end of knowledge. So why write more holy books, open more schools, preserve more teachings? The burning up inside you of everything you want is the meaning of ashes. When you know nothing, you say a lot. When you know something, there's nothing to say.

* * * * *

I cannot form any image at any time. It does not matter here whether the eyes are open or closed. The only thing that is there in that individualized consciousness is the sure reflection of what is presented to it. You do not name it. The movement or desire to know what it is, is simply is not there. The explanations don't mean a thing. That is why I maintain that your natural state is one of not knowing.

We have superimposed a naming process over this natural physiological awareness, an awareness we share, incidentally, with the other animals. Awareness and the movement or tendency in you to bring about change in you are two different things entirely. That difference cannot be perceived by you for there is no perception without the perceiver. Can you become conscious of anything except through the medium of memory and thought? Memory is knowledge. Even your feelings are memory. The stimulus and the response form one unitary movement. They cannot be neatly separated.

In other words, you cannot even differentiate the stimulus from the response. There is no dividing line except when thought steps in and creates one. Thought, as memory and knowledge, has created this mechanism. The only way it can perpetuate itself is to gather knowledge, to know more and more, to ask more and more questions. As long as you are seeking you will be asking questions, and the questioning mechanism only adds more momentum to the naming process.

Thought can never capture the movement of life, it is much too slow. It is like lightning and thunder. They occur simultaneously but sound, traveling slower than light, reaches you later, creating the illusion of two separate events. It is only the natural physiological sensations and perceptions that can move with the flow of life. There is no question of capturing or containing that movement. We like to use the word consciousness glibly, as if we are intimately familiar with it. Actually, consciousness is something we will never know.

As far as I am concerned, we become conscious of something only through memory, knowledge. Otherwise, space and the separative consciousness it creates are not there. There is no such thing as looking at something without the interference of knowledge. To look you need space, and thought creates that space. So space itself, as a dimension, exists only as a creation of thought. Thought has also tried to theorize about the space it has created, inventing the time-space continuum. Time is an independent reference or frame. There is no necessary continuity between it and space.

Thought has also invented the opposite of time, the now, the eternal now. The present exists only as an idea. The moment you attempt to look at the present it has already been brought into the framework of the past. Thought will use any trick under the sun to give momentum to its own continuity. Its essential technique is to repeat the same thing over and over again. This gives it an illusion of permanency. This permanency is shattered the moment the falseness of the past-present-future continuum is seen. The future can be nothing but the modified continuity of the past.

* * * * *

Nature cannot be captured by thought. The important thing to see is the false separation between you and nature. Thought has created all these divisions, making what you call experience possible. The man who has freed himself from all divisions in consciousness has no experiences. He does not have loving relationships, does not question anything, has no notions about being a self-realized man and is not stuck on wanting to help somebody else. What I am maintaining is that the whole problem has been created by culture. It is that that has created this neurotic division in man. Somewhere along the line, man separated himself and experienced self-consciousness, which the other animals don't have, for the first time. This has created misery for man. That is the beginning of the end of man.

The individual who is able through luck to be free from this self-consciousness is no longer experiencing an independent existence. He is, even to himself, like any other thing out there. What happens in the environment repeats itself within such an individual without the knowledge. Once thought has burnt itself out, nothing that creates division can remain there. While thought is taking birth, the disintegration or death of thought is taking place also. That is why it is not natural for thought to take root. Only by maintaining a divisive consciousness in man is thought capable of denying the harmonious functioning of the body. To cast man in religious or psychological terms is to deny the extraordinary intelligence of this wondrous body. It is the movement of thought that is constantly taking you away from your natural state and creating this division.

Is there any way for us to experience, much less share, reality? Forget about ultimate reality, you have no way of experiencing the reality of anything. Experiencing reality from moment to moment is also a thought-induced state of mind. Without a common reference point, which is another invention of thought, how can you communicate and share? It is just not possible. There is nothing to communicate anyhow. You want to use communication to help you out of the mess you are in. That is your only interest. Getting out of your situation is your only aim. Why? Why do you want to get out of your situation? Wanting to get out of situations is what has created the problem in the first place. Wanting to free yourself from the burden is really the problem.

I am not recommending anything. Doing or not doing lead to the same end, misery. So doing nothing is no different from doing something. As long as you have knowledge about that burden, which I deny exists, you will have to struggle to be free of it. You cannot do otherwise. Anything you do is part of the mechanism of thought. Your search for happiness is prolonging your unhappiness. What is there inside you is only the movement of knowledge wanting to know more and more. The you, the separative structure, can continue only as long as there is a demand to know.

* * * * *

The demand for freedom, whether outwardly or inwardly, has been with us for a long while. We have been told that this demand is a sacred, noble thing. Have we again been misled? The demand to be free is the cause of your problems. You want to see yourself as free. The one that is saying, You are not free, is the same one that is telling you that there is a state of freedom to be pursued. But the pursuit is slavery, the very denial of freedom. I do not know anything about freedom because I do not know anything about myself, free, enslaved, or otherwise.

Freedom and self-knowledge are linked. Since I do not know myself and have no way of seeing myself except by the knowledge given me by my culture, the question of wanting to be free does not arise at all. The knowledge you have about freedom denies the very possibility of freedom. When you stop looking at yourself with the knowledge you have, the demand to be free from that self drops away.

What is there is the constant demand to be free. Nothing else is there. How can you, and why should you, be free from memory? Memory is absolutely essential. The problem is not having a memory but your tendency to use memory to further your spiritual interests or as a means to find happiness. To attempt to be free from memory is withdrawal, and withdrawal is death.

* * * * *

The greatest ideal, the most imposing, perfect and powerful, is, of course, God. It is an invention of frightened minds. The human mind has many destructive inventions to its credit. The most destructive one, and the one that has corrupted you, is the invention of God. The history of human thinking has produced saints, teachers, gurus, but God is the most corrupt of them all. Man has already messed up his life and religion has made it worse. It is religion that really made a mess of man's life.

* * * * *

What I am trying to say is that there is no individual there at all. There is only a certain gathering of knowledge, which is thought, but no individuality there. The knowledge you have of things is all that you are capable of experiencing. Without knowledge, no experience of any kind is possible. You cannot separate experience and knowledge. The self is nothing sacred. It is the totality of your knowledge and you are, unfortunately, stuck with it. Why are you interested in separating the knowledge you have about yourself, whatever you call yourself? Knowledge is all that is there. Where is the self? It is an illusion.

Similarly, enlightenment has no independent existence of its own apart from your knowledge about it. There is no enlightenment at all. The idea of illumination is tied up with change but there is nothing to change. Change admits of time. Change always takes time. To change, to eliminate one thing and replace it with another, takes time. What you are now and what you ought to be are linked together by time. You are going to be enlightened tomorrow.

Let us take this as an example. You want to be enlightened. You want to be selfless. You are this, you want to be that. The gap between the two is filled with time. Your enlightenment or selflessness is always tomorrow, not now. So time is essential and time is thought. Your thought structure, which is you, can't conceive of the possibility of anything happening except in time.

This escapist logic is also applied by everyone to spiritual matters, only the time frame is larger. It happens in heaven or perhaps in a future life, at any rate later. And just as there is no tomorrow in these matters, so its reference point, the present, does not exist. Where does it not exist? In thought, which is the past. There is no question of enlightenment now because there is no now, only the projection of the past.

* * * * *

What I am saying is valid and true for me, that is all. If I suggest anything, directly or indirectly, you will turn it into another method or technique. I would be falsifying myself if I were to make any such suggestion. If anyone says there is a way out he is not an honest fellow. He is doing it for his own self-aggrandizement, you may be sure. He simply wants to market a product and hopes to convince you that it is superior to other products on the market. If another man comes along and says that there is no way out, you make of that another method.

You can't blast what I am saying as long as you are relying upon what someone has said before. The saint is a technocrat. That is what most people are. Don't listen to me, it will create an unnecessary disturbance in you. It will only intensify the neurotic situation you are already caught in. Having taken for granted the validity of all this holy stuff, having never questioned, much less broken away from it, you not only have learned how to live with it but also how to capitalize on it. It is a matter of profiteering, nothing more.

Anything I do to help would only add to your misery, that is all. By continuing to listen to me you merely heap one more misery upon those you already have. In that sense, this discussion we are having is doing you no good whatever. You don't seem to realize that you are playing with fire here. If you really want freedom here and now you can have it.

You see, you are anger, selfishness and all these things. If they go, you go. There is a physical going, not in the abstract but actual, physical death. It can happen now, you simply don't want it. You would not touch it with a ten-foot pole. If anger and selfishness, which is you, go, liberation is now, not tomorrow. Your own anger will burn you, not the fire. The religious man has invented selflessness. If that selflessness goes, you go, that is all.

So freeing yourself from any one of these things implies that you, as you know and experience yourself, are coming to an end now. Please, in your interest and out of compassion, I am telling you that this is not what you want. This is not a thing you can make happen. It is not in your hands at all. It hits whomsoever it chooses. You are out of the picture altogether.

You have to actually touch life at a point where nobody has touched it before. Nobody can teach you that. As long as you continue to repeat what others have said before, you are lost and nothing good can come of it. Listening to and believing what others have said is not the way to find out for yourself and there is no other way.

You may very well ask why the hell I am talking. I emphatically assure you that, in my case, it is not at all in the nature of self-fulfillment. My motive for talking is quite different from what you think it is. It is not that I am eager to help you understand or that I feel that I must help you, not at all. My motive is direct and temporary. You arrive seeking understanding, while I am only interested in making it crystal clear that there is nothing to understand.

As long as you want to understand, so long there will be this awkward relationship between two individuals. I am always emphasizing that somehow the truth has to dawn upon you that there is nothing to understand. As long as you think, accept and believe that there is something to understand, and make that understanding a goal to be placed before you, demanding search and struggle, you are lost and will live in misery. The search is invalid because it is based upon questions which in turn are based upon false knowledge. Your knowledge has not freed you from your problems.

So what is your goal? You must be very clear about it, otherwise there is no point in proceeding. It becomes a game, a meaningless ritual. What do you want to get? There is always somebody to help you get what you want for a price. You have foolishly divided life into higher and lower goals, into material and spiritual paths. In either case, great struggle, pain and effort is involved. I say, on the other hand, that there are no spiritual goals at all. They are simply the extension of material goals to what you imagine to be a higher, loftier plane.

You mistakenly believe that by pursuing the spiritual goal you will somehow miraculously make your material goals simple and manageable. Such pursuits are in actuality not possible. You may think that only inferior persons pursue material goals, that material achievements are boring. But, in fact, the so-called spiritual goals you have put before yourself are exactly the same. You are your search.

* * * * *

The past will always be there as long as you want something. Even if you attempt to suppress your wants, the past has to come to your help and tell you how to suppress your wants. There is no such differentiation of wants. They are all exactly the same. When wanting ceases even for a moment thought is absent and you are left with the simple matter of taking care of the bodily needs" food, clothes and shelter.

If you go on trying to suppress the past, trying to live in what you call the present, you will drive yourself crazy. You are trying to control something over which you have no control. It is just not possible to control thought without becoming neurotic, for it is not just your personal, petty little past that is in the way but the entire past of mankind, the entire memory of every human being, every form of life and every form of existence. It is not such a simple, easy thing to do.

If you try to control the natural flow of the river through all these artificial means, building a dam, so to speak, you will inundate and destroy the whole thing. That is why you find thoughts welling up inside you despite your efforts to control, observe and be aware of them. Once this is understood then you are never concerned whether thoughts are there or not.

When there is an actual need for thought to function, it is there. When there is no need for thought to function, it is not there. You don't even know and have no way of finding out whether you are thinking or not. Your constant utilization of thought to give continuity to your separative self is you. There is nothing there inside you other than that.

What you call the self is nothing other than the continuity of thought. If that artificial continuity is not there, neither are you. The self wants only to function on a different, higher level and not to come to an end. You want to be transformed, to become something else, while continuing. The only way the self can do that is to add more and more experiences to those it has already accumulated.

Whether you want something material or simple peace of mind, it makes no difference. As long as you are searching for peace of mind, you will have a tormented mind. If you try not to search or if you continue to search you will remain the same. You have to stop. You don't stop searching because such an act would be the end of you.

You are lost in a jungle and you have no way of finding your way out. Night is fast approaching. The wild animals are there including the cobras and still you are lost. What do you do in such a situation? You just stop. You don't move. As long as there is that hope that you can somehow or the other get out of the jungle, so long will you continue what you are doing, searching, and so long you feel lost. You are lost only because you are searching. You have no way of finding your way out of the jungle.

You still expect something to happen. That expectation is part of the problem. Your expectations are part of your desire to change everything. Nothing needs changing. You must accept life as it is. You may as well find out if it is possible to be at peace now. You want so many things and I am not in a position to help you get any of them. You are not clear what you really want. When that which you want is fully recognized then you find out how to get it and either you get it or you don't, that's all. Don't bother separating your goals into the low and the lofty. You have been doing that all your life and have not succeeded.

* * * * *

When once you have understood that there is nothing to understand, what is there to communicate? Communication is just not necessary. Your desire to communicate is part of your general strategy of achievement. Veiled behind that desire for communication is the dependency upon some outside power to solve your problems for you. Except for the quite natural need for practical communication necessary to function in this world, your interest in communication is really an expression of your feelings of helplessness and your hope for the support of some outside agency.

Your helplessness persists because of your dependency upon some outside agency. When that dependency, fictitious or not, is not there then the feelings of helplessness and the desire to communicate in the abstract are not there. If the one goes, the other must go also. Your situation and prospects only seem hopeless because you have ideas of hope. There is bound to be helplessness and overwhelming frustration as long as you exist in relationship with the hope for fulfillment because there is no fulfillment at all. This is the source of your dilemma.

* * * * *

The future is created by hope. That is the only future that exists. The hope of achieving your goal, the hope of attaining enlightenment, the hope of somehow getting off the merry-go-round "that is the future. The point from which you project yourself into the future appears to you to be the present, the now, but this is mistaken. There is only the past in operation and that movement creates the illusion of present and future. You may find what I am saying here logical or illogical and you may accept or reject it. But it will, in any case, be the past that is doing so for that is all that is in operation within you.

It is the past that has projected these goals "God, enlightenment, peace of mind, whatever" and has placed them in the future out of reach. There is only the past. You have been told by holy men who talk of enlightenment and such nonsense that the past has got to come to a stop before you are free to operate in the present and so realize your potential or future possibilities. This I deny.

First of all, why should you be interested in attempting to stop the past from interfering with the present? Be very clear that this idea that the past must die, that time must have an end, has been put into you by those self-appointed guardians of your so-called soul "the priests, holy men and saviors of mankind. It is not yours at all. You need to be very clear also about the implications of ending the influence of the past. It is really a dangerous, calamitous thing.

In your search to find the end of time, the past, you must use the past, so you only succeed in perpetuating the past. This is a fact, like it or not. Anything you do "having kinder thoughts, behaving selflessly, approaching life negatively rather than positively, listening to holy men, listening to me" is only adding momentum to the past. All the techniques and methods of achievement at your disposal are from the past and, therefore, useless. Luckily, there is absolutely nothing to be achieved.

Your actual approach to happiness is grounded in self-interest and naivet. To demand the cessation of the continuity of the movement of the past is ridiculous and unfounded. We have been brainwashed that if we free ourselves from the past everything will be hunky-dory, full of lightness and sweetness. It is all romantic hogwash" sheer unadulterated fantasy and nothing more.

All your actions are from the past and anything you do only strengthens the hold of pleasure and pain upon you. Ultimately, it is all pain and no pleasure. I can say that with certainty but you are still cocksure that there is a timeless state, a way out. It is therefore impossible for us to communicate. What I am saying will, if really listened to, put an end to you as you know and experience yourself. You are not listening to me at all. Your so-called listening is all in the past. The constant interpretation by the past of what is being said prevents you from listening to what is being said.

All I can guarantee you is that as long as you are searching for happiness you will remain unhappy. This is a fact. Society is so organized and complex that you have no other way of surviving except to accept the way of life around you along with the limitations it places upon all of us. We must all accept the reality of society whether we like it or not. All your relationships, knowledge and experiences, all your emotions and feelings, all that romantic stuff, belongs entirely to society, not to you.

You are not an individual at all. Only when you are free from what every man and woman has thought and felt before you will you become an individual. Such an individual will not burn books that men have made with great care. He would not be a rebel. All the accumulated knowledge, experience and suffering of mankind is inside of you. You must build a huge bonfire within you. Then you will become an individual. There is no other way.

* * * * *

You want to change yourself into something and at the same time find you cannot change at all. This change you talk of is really just more romantic, fancy stuff for you. You never change, only think about changing. As long as you want to change for some reason or the other so long will you insist upon changing the whole world. You want a different world so that you can be happy in it. That is your only interest. You can talk of mankind "concern for mankind, compassion for mankind" but it is all bullshit.

Since you are determined to bring about change, a notion put into you by your culture, you remain discontent and want the world to be different. When your inner demand to be something different from what in fact you are comes to an end then the neurotic demand to change your society ceases. Then you cannot be in conflict with society. You are in perfect harmony with society, including its brutalities and miseries. All your attempts to change this brutal society only add momentum to it.

This is not to say that the free individual is indifferent to society, on the contrary. In any case, it is you who are indifferent right now. You only talk and whine, meanwhile doing nothing. Unless you are at peace with yourself there cannot be peace around the world. When you are at peace with yourself that is the end of the story.

* * * * *

You are trying to establish relationships with people around you, with society, with the whole world. For some reason or other, the actual relationships are very ugly and horrible. Have you noticed that as long as our relationships can be directed to serve personal happiness there is no conflict? Every person is in the same situation. Relationships are harmonious as long as they serve one's ideas of happiness. Because you cannot face the dynamism of relationships you invent sentiments, romance and dramatic emotions to give them continuity. Therefore, you are always in conflict.

* * * * *

Understanding yourself is one of the greatest jokes perpetrated on the gullible and credulous people everywhere, not only by the purveyors of ancient wisdom, the holy men, but also by the modern scientists. The psychologists love to talk about self-knowledge, self-actualization, living from moment to moment and such rot. These absurd ideas are thrown at us as if they are something new.

* * * * *

I have been everywhere in the world meeting and talking with people. People are exactly the same the world over. The questions never vary but I am never bored with it. How can I be bored? If I were some sort of fool getting some sort of kick out of this, looking for new, better and different questions then there would be a possibility of getting bored. But I am not looking for anything so boredom is impossible.

* * * * *

You are alive because your parents had sex, period. Don't look for a meaning to life. There may not be any meaning at all. It may have its own meaning that you can never know. Obviously, life has no meaning for you, otherwise you would not be here asking these questions. Everything you do seems absolutely meaningless. That is the fact. Don't bother about others. The whole world is an extension of you. The way you are thinking, feeling and experiencing is exactly the same way everyone else in this world is thinking, feeling and experiencing.

The goal may be different but the mechanism and instrument you are using to achieve your particular goal is not a whit different from that used by others to achieve theirs. Why should there be any meaning in living? The moment a baby arrives in the world it is interested in one thing, survival. The instinct in the baby to feed itself, to survive and to reproduce itself, seems to be the way of life. It is life expressing itself, that is all. You needn't impose a meaning upon it.

Instead of living you are obsessed with the question, How am I to live? That dilemma is put into us by our culture and is the one responsible for many of our problems. Because you are dead, not living what we call life, you are concerned with how to live. If you succeed in getting rid of the idea of somehow living a better, nobler and more meaningful life you will replace that belief with another. You must face the fact that you know nothing about life or the living of it.

* * * * *

I am just singing my song then I go. If someone listens to me or not it is not my concern. If nobody comes and talks it is alright with me. Believe me, my talking is only incidental. It is not aimed at liberating anyone. If you are not here it's all the same for me. I am not selling anything. I am simply pointing out that at the rate at which we are going the whole genetic engineering technology will end up in the hands of the political system to be used for the complete control and subjugation of man.

This natural state cannot be used to further anyone's crusade nor am I interested in setting myself up as an archetype or prophet for mankind. I am not interested in satisfying the curiosity of anybody. The scientists are making tremendous progress in the fields of microbiology and glandular and brain physiology. They will soon have enough sophistication in these areas to understand the physiological mutation that took place within me. I personally cannot make any definite statement except to say that the whole mechanism is an automatic thing. The interference of thought is not there anymore.

Thought is functional in value, nothing more. It operates temporarily here when there is a demand from the environment but cannot act with regard to becoming something or to changing things there. That is energy, an energy that can make functioning in this world sanely and intelligently an easy affair. Now you are wasting that energy by attempting to be something other than what you, in fact, are. Then you will have a certainty which cannot be transmitted by me or by anybody.

I have discovered, for myself and by myself, that what we have been told about freedom, enlightenment and God is false. No power in the world can touch this. This does not make me superior, nothing of the sort. To feel superior or inferior you must separate yourself from the world. I do not look upon the world as a separate thing, as you do. The knowledge I have about the world, whether within or without, comes into operation only when there is a demand for it. Otherwise, I simply don't know.

Your natural state is one of not knowing. The knowledge that you are this, that you are that, that you are happy, that you are unhappy, that you are a realized man, that you are not a realized man, is completely absent here. We have no way of knowing if we are free. Nothing tells me that I am free. In your case, the naming process, the wanting something, the questioning, goes on and on no matter what.

Here thought functions only from a stimulus from the outside. Even then, the response of knowledge is instantaneous and I am back again like a big question mark. Your constant demand to experience the same thing over and over again results in compulsive, repetitive thinking. I don't see any need or reason for the repetitive process to go on and on.

In my case, there is no one separate from this functioning, no one who can step back and say, "This is reality." There is no such thing as reality at all. Reality is imposed upon us by culture, society and education. Don't get me wrong, thought has a functional value. If we don't accept the world as it is imposed on us we will end up in the loony bin. I have to accept it as a relative fact. Otherwise, there is no way of experiencing the reality of anything.

It is thought that has created the reality of your body, of your living, of your sleep, and of all your perceptions. You experience this reality through knowledge. Otherwise, there is no way of your knowing for yourself that you have a body, that you are alive, that you are awake. All that is knowledge. The reality of anything is something which cannot be experienced by anybody.

* * * * *

The military wars out there are the extension of what is going on all the time inside you. Why is there a war waging inside you? Because you search for peace. The instrument you are using in your attempt to be at peace with yourself is war. There is already peace in man. You need not search. The living organism is functioning in an extraordinarily peaceful way.

Man's search for truth is born out of this same search for peace. It only ends up disturbing and violating the peace that is already there in the body. So what we are left with is the war within and the war without. It's an extension of the same thing. Our search in this world for peace, being based upon warfare, will lead only to war, towards damnation. Humanity has polluted, destroyed and killed off everything, all on account of his wanting to be at the center of the universe, of all creation.

* * * * *

You are interested in the self, not I. Whatever it is, it is the most important thing for man as long as he is alive. If you don't think it never occurs to you that you are alive or dead. The very birth of thought creates fear and it is out of fear that all experience springs. Both inner and outer worlds proceed from a point of thought. Everything you experience is born out of thought.

So everything you experience or can experience is an illusion. The self-absorption in thought creates a self-centeredness in man "that is all that is there. All relationships based upon that will inevitably create misery for man. These are bogus relationships. As far as you are concerned, there is no such thing as a relationship. And yet, society demands not just relationships but permanent relationships.

* * * * *

It is mortality that creates immortality. It is the known that creates the unknown. It is time that has created the timeless. It is thought that created the thoughtless. Just as we all breathe from a common fund of air we appropriate and use thoughts to function in this world. Man's insistence that thought must be continuous denies the nature of thought, which is short-lived. Thought has created for itself a separate destiny. It has been very successful in creating for itself a separate parallel existence. By positing the unknown, the beyond, the immortal, it has created for itself a way to continue on.

There is no timeless, only time. When thought creates time, a space is created there. So thought is space as well. Thought also creates matter; no thought no matter. Thought is a manifestation or expression of life and to make of it a separate thing, impute to it a life of its own and then allow it to create a future for its own unobstructed continuity, is man's tragedy.

* * * * *

I don't think that this kind of life exists anywhere else on any other planet. I am not saying that there may not be life in other worlds only that it is not like our existence here. Your ruminations about other forms of life and other worlds is just a wish for unlimited extension into the future and far-off places. Thought is trying to give itself continuity and speculating about the future and undiscovered worlds is a convenient way to do it.

* * * * *

In order to concentrate or focus on one thing you must block out the others. By concentrating upon what you take to be nothing you withdraw and separate yourself from the natural flow of life through and around you. You are part of a generalized magnetic field and what separates you from others is thought. You are concerned only with your happiness and unhappiness, the video set you are watching. You view and experience things from a different viewpoint than others, that's all. You think that you are having a subjective experience of an objective thing. There is nothing there, only your relative, experiential data, your truth. There is no such thing as objective truth at all. There is nothing which exists outside or independent of our minds.

That part of culture that promises you peace, bliss, heaven and selflessness is the problem. To separate the rest of culture "how you entertain yourself, how you eat, your work habits and language" from this counter-reality created by culture is a mistake. The so-called savages are functioning in exactly the same way we are functioning today. Basically, there is no difference. In either the primitive or modern cultures there is no peace.

The idea that there is peace somewhere else, sometime in the future, is causing the problem. All these religious experiences like compassion, bliss and love are part of the craving for a non-existent peace which is destructive to the natural peace already there. Whatever is happening at the moment is all that there is for me. All your yesterdays, all your knowledge and your very sense of self are dead things of the past. These memories have a great deal of emotional content for you but not for me. I am only interested in what is actually happening now, not tomorrow or yesterday.

I have no particular message for mankind nor do I have any of the missionary zeal in me. I am not a savior of mankind or any such thing. People come here out of their own free will and volition because they have heard of me or out of sheer curiosity, it doesn't matter. A person may come here out of any one of a number of reasons. He finds me somehow different, a rare bird, and cannot figure me out or fit me into any framework he knows. He tells his friends and soon they arrive at the door. I can't tell them to get lost. I invite them in knowing very well that there is nothing I can do for them. What can I do for you? "Come in, sit down, make yourself comfortable," is all I can say.

* * * * *

Whatever happens, it changes the movement and demands your complete attention. Everything happening at that moment demands your complete and total attention. In that state there are no longer two things; lover and beloved, pursuer and pursued. What you call a beautiful woman, which is an idea, gives way to something else.

Romanticism is not my reality. Nothing has ever or will ever sweep me off my feet. It is not that I am the opposite of that, a man of reason. It is the element of reason in me that revolted against itself. You may infer a rational meaning in what I say or do but it is your doing not mine. I am not interested in anyone's search for happiness, romance or escape.

There is no experience here. So how can there be these dramatic, crazy experiences? I have no way of separating myself from events. The event and I are one and the same. I have no teaching. There is nothing to preserve. Teaching implies something that can be used to bring about change. Sorry, there is no teaching here, just disjointed, disconnected sentences. What is there is only your interpretation, nothing else. For this reason there is not now nor will there ever be any kind of copyright for whatever I am saying. I have no claims.

* * * * *

My mother died when I was seven days old. My maternal grandparents took care of me. My grandfather was a Theosophist. He was a wealthy man and instilled a strong religious atmosphere around the house. So in that sense, J. Krishnamurti was also part of my background. They had his pictures, I could not avoid him. I did not go to him in search of anything. He was just part of my background. It would have been remarkable had I never gone to see him. My problem was to free myself from the whole background that was strangling me, that's all.

It is like the man who is riding a tiger and is thrown off. The tiger, maintaining its own momentum, continues on. It's gone. That's all there is to it. You cannot do anything with the tiger anymore. You never again have the fear of encountering or riding the tiger. It is finished. It has gone. So I think there is little point in my doing anything in society. It has its own momentum. Anything you try to do will engulf you and add to that momentum. Who has given the mandate to all these people to save mankind?

* * * * *

If the entire collective knowledge and experience of man is thrown out, what is left is a primordial and primeval state, without the primitiveness. That kind of individual is of no use to society at all. Like a shady tree, this individual may provide shade but can never be conscious of his doing so. If you sit under the tree a coconut may fall on your head. There is a danger involved. For this reason, society may feel threatened by this individual. This society, structured the way it is, can make no use of such a person.

When once the organism has freed itself from the stranglehold of thought, anything you do to try to bring about peace and harmony there only creates disharmony and violence. It is like using war to create peace in a peaceful world. When the search itself comes to an end it comes to an end with a big bang, as it were. Then peace is something that cannot be practiced or taught.

If you drop the fictitious models of the saint and holy man you are left with the natural biological arrangement. The separative structure of thought which was introduced into the consciousness of man long ago has created the violent world and will probably push man and the rest of life on this planet to the brink of extinction. But biologically, each cell has the wisdom to avoid models and promises and simply, out of sheer survival motives, cooperates with the cell next to it. Out of the terror of annihilation, man, like the cells of his body, will learn to cooperate, but not out of love or compassion.

* * * * *

The control of the body through thought has destroyed the possibility of growing into complete humans. The extraordinary intelligence of the biological organism is all that is necessary for good living but we are all the time interfering with its natural operation through the medium of thought. Your natural bodily computer is already programmed. You don't have to do a thing. Somehow, you see, something hits you like lightning and burns the whole thing there. This man then is neither sinner nor saint. He is far outside the framework of society.

For forty-nine years I searched for a man called U.G. The whole culture put me on the wrong track. I tried the dead gurus as well as the living ones. Eventually I realized that the search was useless, that the enemy was me. Now the entire knowledge and the search it engendered has been thrown out of my system completely. The demand to change one's self and the demand to change the world go out of the system together. I am neither antisocial nor thankful to society. I don't feel any bounden duty to play any part or to help my fellow men. All this kind of thing is balderdash.

The man who is trying to free himself from the world or from what he calls evil is actually the most egotistical of men. The shattering perception that finally dawns on you is that there is no such thing as ego at all. This insight blows everything apart with a tremendous force when it hits you. It is not an experience that can be shared with another. It is not an experience at all. It is a calamity in which both experience and the experiencer come to an end. A man in such a state does not escape reality and has no romantic tendencies. He harbors no humanistic notions about saving the world for he knows that anything that is done to save it only adds momentum to it. He knows that there is nothing you can do.

Your actions and the consequences of those actions form one single event. It is the logical, cause and effect thinking that imposes a sequence to events. The sudden evidence of light and the throwing of the light switch which preceded it are actually one thing, not two. They appear to you as two or more events only because time has created a space between. But time and space, apart from the ideas of time and space, do not exist at all.

Creation and destruction are going on simultaneously. The birth and death of thought happen simultaneously. That is why I insist that there is no such thing as death at all. Even the body does not die. It can change form but does not cease altogether. Because death really does not exist it is impossible for you to experience it. What you do experience is the void or emptiness you feel upon the disappearance of someone's body. Death can never be experienced and neither can birth for that matter. In your natural state, where the body is allowed to function without the interference of thought, birth and death are going on all the time.

There is no person and no space within to create a self. What is left after the continuity of thought is blown away is one disjointed and independent series of interactions. What happens in the environment around me happens in here. There is no division. When the armor you are wearing around you is stripped away, you find an extraordinary sensitivity of the senses that responds to the phases of the moon, the passage of the seasons and the movements of the other planets. There is simply no isolated, separate existence of its own here, only the throb of life.

In this death state, the ordinary breath stops entirely and the body is able to breathe through other physiological means. Among the many doctors I have discussed this strange phenomenon with only one expert in childbirth gave me a sort of explanation. He says that newborn babies have a similar way of breathing. This death process is yoga, not the hundreds of postures and breathing exercises. When the thought process stops splitting itself in two, the body goes through a clinical death. First, the death must take place then yoga begins.

Yoga is actually the body's skill in bringing itself back from the state of clinical death. This yoga of renewal is an extraordinary thing. If you observe a newborn baby you will have observed the way it moves and articulates its whole body all in a natural rhythm. After the breath and heartbeat come to an almost complete stop somehow the body begins to come back. The corpse-like appearance of the body "the stiffness, coldness and ash covering" begins to disappear, the body warms up and begins to move and the metabolism including the pulse picks up.

So it is much more like the Tai Chi than classical yoga postures. The movements and postures that the body performs when breaking down the stiffness left over from the death process are beautiful, graceful movements, like those of a newborn baby. Yogis now prescribe savasana, the corpse posture, after the performance of any moving postures. This is backwards. You start yoga as a dead stiff body then the body is renewed through natural rhythmic movements.

This whole process of dying and being renewed, although it happens to me daily and without my volition, remains very intriguing to me. It just happens out of nowhere. Even the thought of the self or ego has been annihilated. Still, there is something there experiencing this death, otherwise I would not be able to describe it here.

With the absence of any demand to repeat or use this death process the senses are given a field day. The breath, no longer under the domination of the separative thought structure, can respond fully to the physical environment. Upon seeing a beautiful mountain or sunset, the breath is suddenly drawn out of you then back in, all in a natural rhythm. This is where the expression, breathtaking beauty, probably comes from.

The only way you become conscious of things happening around you is through subtle changes in breathing patterns. It is a tremendous mechanism and in it there are no persons, no things. Sometimes you are just sitting there and you suddenly feel a shortness of breath, almost a gasping for air. It is something like a second wind. But even this passes and finally breathing stops altogether and the body bypasses the lungs, breathing with the pulse of the body alone.

One paper stresses the difference in the way my thymus gland functions. But there are other glands that are affected also "the pineal, the pituitary and others. The pineal gland, which controls the whole movement, breathing and coordination of the body, is greatly affected. When the separative thought structure dies these glands and nerve plexuses take over the functioning of the organism.

It is a painful process, for the hold of thought over the glands and plexuses is strong and has to be burnt off. This can be experienced by an individual. The burning or ionization needs energy and space to take place. For this reason, the limits of the body are reached, with energy lashing out in all directions. The body's containment of that energy in its limited form brings pain even though there is no experiencer of pain there. This painful death process is something nobody wants, not even the most ardent religious practitioners and yogis.

It is not the result of will but of a fortuitous concourse of atoms. How all this fits into your scientific structure, I do not know. Scientists doing work in this field are interested in these changes if they are described in physiological rather than mystical terms. These scientists envisage this kind of man as representing the end product of biological evolution, not the science-fiction superman or super spiritual beings. Nature is only interested in creating an organism that can respond fully and intelligently to stimuli and reproduce itself, that's all. This body is capable of extraordinary perceptions and sensations. It is a marvel.

Scientists in the field of evolution now think that the present breed of humans we have on this planet probably evolved out of a degenerated species. The mutation that carried on the self-consciousness must have taken place in a degenerate species. That is why we have messed everything up. It is anybody's guess as to whether anyone can change the whole thing. I think that human consciousness in its totality is a tremendously powerful thing with a strong momentum of its own. The whole of human consciousness is a very formidable thing.

The scientific procedure, not the self, gives you a reference point so that you may measure the truth or falseness of what I am saying. Look, I tried everything to find an answer to my burning obsession, Is there such a thing as enlightenment at all or have we all been fooled by abstractions? The utter frustration and complete failure to answer that question created an intensity.

The first part of my life was spent in India around yogis, holy men, sages; in short, all the associations that could benefit a person interested in spiritual matters. I found out for myself that it was all bogus. There was nothing to it at all. Totally disillusioned with the whole religious traditions of both the East and the West, I plunged myself into modern psychology, science and whatever the material world could give me.

I found out for myself that the whole idea of spirit or psyche was false. When I experimented with and studied the material world, I was surprised to find that there was no such thing as matter at all. Denying the spiritual and material basis of things, I was left with nowhere to turn. I began drifting on my own, unable to find an answer from any source.

Then one day the futility of what I was doing dawned upon me and the question which had obsessed me for almost my entire life got burnt then disappeared. After that there were no more questions. The thirst burned itself out without ever satisfying itself. Not answers but the ending of questions is the important thing. Even though everything got burnt there, still embers remain to express themselves in a natural rhythm. What impact this expression may have on the society around me is not my concern.

There is no self, there is no I, there is no spirit, there is no soul and there is no mind. That knocks off the whole list and you have no way of finding out what you are left with. You may very well ask me the question, Why do you go on telling people about the way you are functioning? It is only to emphasize that we have been for centuries using some instrument, that is, thinking or mind or whatever you want to call it to free ourselves from the whole of what you call the self and all kinds of things. That is what the whole quest of spirit is all about. But once it dawns on you that there is nothing to be free from then these questions don't arise at all. How that dawned on me I have no way of finding out for myself.

The answers I give are only to emphasize that what we are left with is the functioning of the living organism. How it is functioning is all that I am trying to put across, emphasize and overemphasize all the time. My interest is to somehow make you see that the whole attempt on your part to understand what you are left with is a lost battle. Even that statement cannot be experienced by what is left there. When once the whole thing is flushed out of your system, the statement, "We are left with only the physical body and the universe that statement also cannot stand any more.

The more the questions you throw at me the more there is a need to emphasize the physical aspect of our existence, namely, that there is nothing to what we have been made to believe. All our problems have arisen because of our acceptance that it is possible for us to understand the reality of the world or the reality of our existence. What I am saying is that you have no way of experiencing anything that you do not know. So anything that you experience through the help of your knowledge is fruitless. It is a lost battle.

That is the reason why I say that the instrument which we are using to understand the reality of our existence and the reality of the world around us is not part of this mechanism that is there. That is the reason why I say thoughts are not self-generated and are not spontaneous. There are no thoughts there even now. If you want to find out whether there is any such thing as thought, the very question which we are posing to ourselves, namely, "Is there a thought?," is born out of the assumption that there is a thought there. But what you will find there is all about thought and not thought. All about thought is what is put in there by the culture. That is put in by the people who are telling us that it is very essential for you to free yourself from whatever you are trying to free yourself from through that instrument.

My interest is to emphasize that that is not the instrument and there is no other instrument. And when once this hits you, dawns upon you, that thought is not the instrument and that there is no other instrument, then there is no need for you to find out if any other instrument is necessary. There is no need for any other instrument. This very same structure that we are using, the instrument which we are using, has in a very ingenious way invented all kinds of things like intuition, right insight, right this, that and the other. And to say that through this very insight we have come to understand something is the stumbling block. All insights however extraordinary they may be are worthless because it is thought that has created what we call insight and through that it is maintaining its continuity and status quo.

* * * * *

I question consciousness because what we call consciousness is memory. You become conscious of something through the help of the knowledge you have and that knowledge is locked up in the memory. So the whole talk of the subconscious, unconscious, levels of consciousness and all that is the ingenious invention of the thinking mechanism. Through this cleverness, inventiveness, it maintains its continuity.

Awareness has no meaning to me because awareness is not an instrument to be used to understand anything, much less to bring about a change there. First of all, there is nothing there to be changed. Since there is nothing there to be changed, whether you use awareness or any other instrument to bring about a change is irrelevant. Awareness can never be separated from the activity of the brain. That is the reason why I always describe what is happening here in physical terms.

What is there is only the reflection of this object on the retina. Even this statement cannot be experienced by me because the stimulus and response are one unitary movement. The moment you say there is awareness, there is already a division. That is the only way you can continue, otherwise you are coming to an end. The you as you know yourself, the you as you experience yourself "that you is the identity there. Through the constant demand for using memory it maintains its continuity. If that you is not there you don't know what will happen.

Thinking cannot help us to solve living problems. There is no way we can use that to solve human problems. That is why it has failed to solve our problems. It has not touched anything there. All our beliefs have not touched anything there. We don't know what we would do in a given situation. You can say that you are going to be a nonviolent man but what you would do in a given situation you would never know. The demand to be prepared for all future actions and situations is the cause of our problems. Every situation is so different and our preparedness to meet that situation with this knowledge we have of answering and dealing with such situations cannot help us.

It is not a challenge. The inadequacy of using what you have, preparing yourself, and the question of how to deal with the situation, are absent here. It ceases to be a challenge then. That is why I say there are no problems there. We create the problems. If the solutions we are offered by those people are really not the solutions you really don't have a problem. But the fact of the matter is if you do not have a problem you create a problem. You cannot live without problems.

This separateness from the totality of things around us and the idea that the whole thing is created for our benefit and that we are created for a grander and nobler purpose than all the other species on this planet are the causes of this destruction. This powerful use of thought is what is destructive. Thought is a self-protective mechanism, so anything that is born out of thought is destructive.

Whether it is religious thought or scientific thought or political thought, all of them are destructive. But we are not ready to accept that it is thought that is our enemy. We don't know how to function in this world without the use of thought. You can invent all kinds of things and try to free yourself from this stranglehold of thought but there is no way we can accept the fact that that is not the instrument to help us to function sanely and intelligently in this world.

Thought is a self-perpetuating mechanism. It controls, molds, shapes our ideas and actions. Idea and action, they are one and the same. All our actions are born out of ideas. Our ideas are thoughts passed on to us from generation to generation. Thought is not the instrument to help us to live in harmony with the life around us. That is why you create all these ecological problems, problems of pollution and the problem of possibly destroying ourselves with the most destructive weapons that we have invented. So, there is no way out. You may say that I am a pessimist, that I am a cynic or that I am this, that and the other. But I hope one day we will realize that the mistakes we have made will destroy everything. The planet is not in danger. We are in danger.

Because you know in a way that what you know of yourself is coming to an end there. You have been through so many experiences. You have achieved so many things. You have attained and accomplished so many things. "Is all that coming to an end, leaving behind nothing?" So naturally we create something beyond. You are not separate from that illusion. You are the illusion. If one illusion goes it is always replaced with another illusion. Why? Because the ending of the illusion is the ending of you. That is the death. The ending of belief is the ending of the you that is there.

We think we know a lot more than this body. We think that we know what is good for that body and that is why we are creating problems for it. It knows what it wants to know. It doesn't want to learn anything from us. If we understand this simple relationship that thought and the body have then probably we will allow the body to function and use thought only for functional purposes. Thought is functional in value and it cannot help us to achieve any of the goals we have placed before us or what the culture has placed before us.

Your value system is the one that is responsible for the human malady, human tragedy, forcing everybody to fit into that model. You may not agree with me, but when we talk about the quest for happiness it is no different from any other sensual activity. As a matter of fact, all experiences, however extraordinary they may be, are in the area of sensuality. That is one major problem that we are facing today.

Somewhere along the line the human species experienced this self-consciousness for the first time and it separated the human species from the rest of the species on this planet. I don't even know if there is any such thing as evolution but we are made to believe that there is such a thing. And it was at that time perhaps that thought took its birth. But thought, in its birth, in its origin, in its content, in its expression, and in its action is very fascist.

When I use the word fascist I use it not in the political sense but to mean that thought controls and shapes our thinking and our actions. So it is a very protective mechanism. It has no doubt helped us to be what we are today. It has helped us to create our high-tech and technology. It has made our life very comfortable. It has also made it possible for us to discover the laws of nature. But thought is a very protective mechanism and is interested in its own survival. At the same time, thought is opposed fundamentally to the functioning of this living organism.

We are made to believe that there is such a thing as mind but there is no such thing as your mind or my mind. Society or culture or whatever you want to call it has created us solely and wholly for the purpose of maintaining its own continuity and status quo. At the same time, it has also created the idea that there is such a thing as the individual. But actually, there is a conflict between the two "the idea of the individual and the impossibility of functioning as an individual separate and distinct from the totality of man's thoughts and experiences.

Here at this point I would like to emphasize that thoughts are not self-generated and spontaneous. I would go one step further and ask, "Is there any such a thing as thought?" The very question arises because we assume that there is such a thing as thought and that we can separate ourselves from thought and look at it. But when we look at what we call thought, what we see is about thought and not thought itself. What is thought?" The question arises only because of the assumption that there is such a thing as thought.

We use what we call thought to achieve our spiritual or material goals. We may consider the spiritual goals as higher. The culture in which we are functioning places spiritual goals on a higher level than the materialistic goals. But the instrument which we are using is matter which is thought. Thought to me is matter. Therefore, all our spiritual goals are materialistic in their value. And this is the conflict that is going on there. In this process, the totality of man's experiences created what we call a separate identity and a separate mind.

But actually, if you want to experience anything, be it your own body or your own experiences, you have no way of experiencing them without the use of the knowledge that is passed on to us. In other words, I would say that thought is memory. But we have been made to believe that human beings are created for a nobler and grander purpose than the other species on this planet and it is that belief that is responsible for our thinking that the whole creation is created for the benefit of man.

Everything that is born out of thought is destructive, anything that we discover. The laws of nature or whatever you call it are used by us only for destructive purposes. And it is true that we have discovered quite a few of nature's laws and the theories are constantly changing. Thought is not the instrument for achieving anything other than the goals set before us by our culture or society or whatever you want to call it. The basic problem we have to face today is this. The cultural input, or what society has placed before us as the goal for all of us to reach and attain, is the enemy of this living organism. Thought can only create problems. It cannot help us to solve any.

What I am talking about is not a thoughtless state. Even the invention of what is called a thoughtless state, placed before us by many spiritual teachers as a goal to be reached, is created by thought so that it can, by pursuing what it calls a thoughtless state, maintain its own continuity. So whatever we experience in this process of achieving the goal of a thoughtless state strengthens and fortifies the very thing that we are trying to be free from.

It is thought that has invented the ideas of cause and effect. There may not be any such thing as a cause at all. Every event is an individual and independent event. We link up all these events and try to create a story of our lives but actually every event is an independent event. If we accept the fact that every event is an independent event in our lives it creates a tremendous problem of maintaining what we call identity. And identity is the most important factor in our lives.

We are able to maintain this identity through the constant use of memory which is also thought. This constant use of memory or identity or whatever you call it is consuming a tremendous amount of energy and it leaves us with no energy to deal with the problems of our living. Is there any way that we can free ourselves from the identity? Through dialectical thinking about thinking itself we are only sharpening that instrument. All philosophies help us only to sharpen this instrument.

Thought is very essential for us to survive in this world but it cannot help us in achieving the goals that we have placed before ourselves. The goals are unachievable through the help of thought. The quest for happiness is impossible because there is no such thing as permanent happiness. There are moments of happiness and there are moments of unhappiness but the demand to be in a permanent state of happiness is the enemy of this body.

This body is interested in maintaining its sensitivity of the sensory perceptions and also the sensitivity of the nervous system. That is very essential for the survival of this body. If we use that instrument of thought for trying to achieve the impossible goal of permanent happiness the sensitivity of this body is destroyed. Therefore, the body is rejecting all that we are interested in "permanent happiness and permanent pleasure. So, we are not going to succeed in that attempt to be in a permanent state of happiness.

Through a repetitive process we are sharpening that instrument but we are using tremendous amounts of energy in this process. If the use of thought is limited to achieve only what we consider to be materialistic values and not our spiritual goals, what is it that is not possible for us in order to function sanely and intelligently? It does not mean that I am teaching a materialistic philosophy or any such thing. Thought is not intended for achieving spiritual goals or even to find out the significance, meaning or purpose of life or to be used for the quest for permanence or permanent pleasure.

* * * * *

A guru is one who tells you to throw away all the crutches that we have been made to believe are essential for our survival. The true guru tells you, Throw them away and don't replace them. You can walk and if you fall you will rise and walk again. Such is the man whom we consider or even tradition considers to be the real guru and not those who are selling those shoddy pieces of goods in the market place today. It is a business It has become a holy business to people.

I am not condemning anything but as long as you depend upon somebody for solving your problems so long you remain helpless. And this helplessness is exploited by the people who actually do not have the answers to your problems but they give you some sort of a comforting. People are satisfied with and fall for this kind of thing instead of dealing with the problems by themselves and for themselves. There is no need for me to free you or enlighten you because to do that I must have an image of myself and in relationship to that an image of you.

To be an individual and to be yourself you don't have to do a thing. Culture demands that you should be something other than what you are. What a tremendous amount of energy we waste trying to become that! If that energy is released what is it that we can't do? How simple it would be for every one of us to live in this world! It is so simple.

The uniqueness of every individual cannot express itself because of the stranglehold of the experiences of others. After all, you don't exist, and I don't exist. You and I have been created by the totality of those experiences, and we have to use them in order to function sanely and intelligently in this world.

* * * * *

It is something like, to use my favorite phrases, lightning hitting you, a jolt of lightning hitting you, and you don't know what you are left with. You have no way of finding out for yourself and by yourself what has happened to you. Has anything happened to me at all? But one thing I can say with certainty is that the very thing that I searched for all my life was shattered to pieces.

The goals that I had set for myself "self-realization, God-realization, transformation, radical or otherwise, or even enlightenment" were all false and there was nothing there to be realized and nothing to be found there. The very demand to be free from anything, even from the physical needs of the body just disappeared and I was left with nothing. Therefore, whatever comes out of me now depends upon what you draw out of me.

I have actually and factually nothing to communicate because there is no communication possible at any level. The only instrument we have is the intellect. We know in a way that this instrument has not helped us to understand anything. So when once it dawns on you that this is not the instrument and that there is no other instrument with which to understand anything you are left with this puzzling situation that there is nothing to understand. In a way it would be highly presumptuous on my part to sit on a platform or accept invitations like this and try to tell people that I have something to say, that I have come into something extraordinary which nobody has come into.

But what I am left with is something extraordinary; extraordinary not in the sense that it has been possible for me through any effort or volition of mine but in the sense that everything that every man thought, felt and experienced before is thrown out of my system. So you can say that it is indeed a courageous thing that has happened to me. But I cannot tell people that through courage you can put yourself into that kind of situation.

It is very difficult to tell people how it all happened to me. They are only interested in finding out how it happened to me because their only interest is to find out the cause, find out what led me into this. But when I tell them that it is acausal it is very difficult for them to understand and accept it. Their interest is to find out a cause and make it happen to them.

You see, when I was listening to J. Krishnamurti it suddenly dawned on me, Why the hell have I been listening to this man? From his description I feel that I am in the same state as that man." I said to myself that I was in the same state as that man, assuming for the moment that he was in the same state that he was describing and in the same state that the great spiritual teachers were in. "What the hell have I been doing all my life? Why the hell am I sitting here listening to him?"

I then walked out with just one single thought whirling in me, as it were, like in a whirlpool. "How do you know that you are in the same state?" I understand that the question implies that I was familiar with the descriptions of various states. I had tried to simulate them in me and experience them and that is all there is to it. So this question went on and on. But suddenly this question also disappeared. I said to myself that there is no reason for me to feel grateful to anybody, to express my thanks to anybody.

Whatever has happened to me has happened despite listening to this teacher or that teacher or doing this, that or the other. But if I say all this it is something which is not very interesting to people. They want to know and I tell them that I myself do not know. I cannot look at myself and tell myself that I am an enlightened man, that I am a free man, that tremendous changes have taken place in me. So I use this phrase which we very often hear on the commercials. It is not something like before and after the wash. No washing has helped me to reach anywhere. It is just a happening. I still have to use the word happening because there is no other way that I can communicate this and give a feel of this to anybody else.

What is reported in the so-called story of my life is a garbled version of what I actually felt at that time. Anyway, anything I say today is irrelevant because I don't know what I felt at that particular moment and there is no way I can relive that experience from here. I said to myself, What is it that he has? If there is anybody in this world who can receive it, it is I." I said this to myself and walked out. That, in a way, decided another phase of my life.

The old traditional approach to the whole question of enlightenment was thrown out of my system although I continued to read books on religion, studied philosophy, psychology and science. I tried to find out answers from those people who have not been contaminated by the traditional teachings. I got interested in Western philosophy and science and tried to find the answer to my basic question.

My basic question was one question, Where is this mind that we are so concerned about, that we are trying to understand, study and change? Why do we talk of a total change in the makeup of the mind? I don't see any such thing as mind there at all, let alone a transformation or mutation of the mind." This question always intrigued me and I questioned everybody about the mind. I tried to get answers from every area of human thought but nothing helped me to find out the answers to those questions. At that time I didn't have the certainty that I have today.

The certainty I have today that there is no mind is something which I cannot transmit to anybody however hard I may try because the very thing which we are using to communicate is in jeopardy and you are not ready to accept that possibility. They made a tremendous structure out of that philosophical thought. They talked of the void. They talked of emptiness. You know, the whole Buddhist philosophy is built on the foundation of that no mind. Yet they have created tremendous techniques of freeing themselves from the mind. All the Zen techniques of meditation try to free you from the mind.

The very instrument that we are using to free ourselves from the thing called mind is the mind. Mind is nothing other than what you are doing to free yourself from the mind. But when it once dawns on you by some strange chance or miracle that the instrument that you are using to understand everything is not the instrument and that there is no other instrument, it hits you like a jolt of lightning.

* * * * *

Do you think these frontiers are going to disappear? They are not. Those who have entrenched themselves, those who have had the monopoly of all the world's resources so far and for so long, if they are threatened to be dislodged, what they would do is anybody's guess. All the destructive weapons that we have today are here only to protect that monopoly.

But I am sure that the day has come for people to realize that all the weapons that we have built so far are redundant and that they cannot be used anymore. We have arrived at a point where you cannot destroy your adversary without destroying yourself. So it is that kind of terror and not the love and brotherhood that have been preached for centuries that will help us to live together.

Until this percolates to the level of human consciousness in the sense that man sees that he cannot destroy his neighbor without destroying himself I don't think it will help. I am sure that we have come to that point. Whenever and wherever you have an edge over your adversary or your neighbor you will still continue to exercise what you have been holding on to for centuries. So how are you going to solve the problem? All utopias have failed.

The whole mischief originated in the religious thinking of man. Now there is no use in blaming the religious thinking of man, because all the political ideologies, even your legal structures, are the warty outgrowth of the religious thinking of man. It is not so easy to flush out the whole series of experiences which have been accumulated through centuries and which are based upon the religious thinking of man. There is a tendency to replace one belief with another belief, one illusion with another illusion. That is all we can do.

Anything that is born out of thought is destructive. You may cover it up with all wonderful and romantic phrases, Love thy neighbor as thyself". Don't forget that in the name of "Love thy neighbor as thyself", millions and millions of people have died, more than in all the recent wars put together. But we now have come to a point where we can realize that violence is not the answer, that it is not the way to solve human problems. So terror seems to be the only way. I am not talking of terrorists blowing up churches, temples and all that kind of thing but the terror that if you try to destroy your neighbor you will possibly destroy yourself. That realization has to come down to the level of the common man.

This is the way the human organism is functioning too. Every cell is interested in its own survival. It knows in some way that its survival depends upon the survival of the cell that is next to it. It is for this reason that there is a sort of cooperation between the cells. That is how the whole organism can survive. It is not interested in utopias. It is not interested in your wonderful religious ideas. It is not interested in peace, bliss, beatitude or anything. Its only interest is to survive. That is all it is interested in. The survival of a cell depends upon the survival of the cell next to it. And your survival and my survival depend upon the survival of our neighbor.

As long as there is division, as long as there is a separation within you, so long do you maintain that separation around you. When everything fails, you use the last card, the trump in the pack of cards, and call it love. But it is not going to help us and it has not helped us at all. Even religion has failed to free man from violence and from ten other different things that it is trying to free us from. You see, it is not a question of trying to find new concepts, new ideas, new thoughts and new beliefs.

The human being modeled after the perfect being has totally failed. That has not touched anything there. Your value system is the one that is responsible for the human malady, the human tragedy "forcing everybody to fit into that model. You cannot do anything by destroying the value system because you replace one value system with another. Even those who rebelled against religion like those in the communist countries have themselves created another kind of value system. Revolution does not mean the end of anything. It is only a revaluation of our value system. The only answer to this human problem, if there is any answer, is not to be found through new ideas, new concepts or new ideologies but through bringing about a change in the chemistry of the human body.

* * * * *

Do you really think that there is freedom in the United States? What does that mean to a starving man "freedom of speech, freedom of worship and freedom of the press? He does not know how to read the newspapers and is not interested in them. At least in the communist systems they fed, clothed and sheltered people, though that is now being denied to them in those nations. There is more unemployment than ever before in the Western countries. I don't think this is the model for the whole of mankind.

The whole system depends upon the exploitation of the resources of the world for the benefit of the Western nations. These laws that you are talking about are always backed by force. Ultimately, it is the force that counts. We all agree to submit ourselves to the decision of the judge. If you don't want to submit to them the only recourse you have is to use violence. So all the gangsters get together and create a legal structure which is favorable to them. That they enforce on others through the help of violence, through the help of force. As long as it is advantageous to you, you talk of law. When the law fails, you use force.

* * * * *

The demand to understand and bring about a change in you is the one that is responsible for the demand to understand the world and then bring about a change in the world. They are one and the same. That is why you are interested in listening to others. Through that listening you think you will be able to bring about a change in you and then also a change in the world around you. Basically, there is no difference between what is here and what is out there in the world. There is no way you can draw a line of demarcation.

One thing that I always emphasize is that it is culture that has created us all for the sole purpose of maintaining its status quo and its continuity. So, in that sense, I do not see that there are any individuals at all. At the same time, the same culture has given us the hope that there is something that you can do to become an individual and that there is such a thing as free will. Actually, there is no free will at all.

The most important thing for us to realize is that thought is a very destructive weapon and that thought is our enemy. However, we are not ready to accept the fact that thought can only create problems but cannot help us to solve them. My point is that there is nothing there to be changed. What these gurus in the marketplace are doing is to sell you some ice packs and provide you with some comforters. But when you come to me you find it very difficult for the simple reason that I do not offer you any solutions to your problems.

My interest is to point out that there are actually no problems, and what we are saddled with are only solutions. Also, we are not ready to accept the fact that the solutions that these people have been offering us for centuries are not really the solutions. If they were really the solutions, the problems would have been solved long ago. If they are not the solutions, and if there are no other solutions, then there are no problems to be solved.

* * * * *

I am afraid that the rise of Islam, not only in the Moslem world but also in Russia and China, is going make it a formidable force. Once this cry of holy war, jihad, spreads around we will not know how to tackle that problem. I am not singing a doomsday song. That is what you are going to face very soon. Islam is going to be a formidable force in the world. I don't know I am not a prophet, I cannot say anything. But like anybody else I can hazard, if I may use the word, a view of the shape of things to come. I don't know for sure and nobody knows, for that matter, what will happen.

There is one thing that I want to say, emphasize, and overemphasize that there is no way we can reverse the whole thing. We are heading towards a disaster. Man must realize, and there seems to be no hope of his coming to terms with the reality of the situation, that thought and all that is born out of our thinking are the enemy of mankind and there is nothing to replace that. Religious revivalism is not really the answer.

I personally feel that the basic question which we all should ask ourselves is, "What kind of a human being you want on this planet?" Unfortunately, culture, whether it is Oriental or Occidental, has placed before us the model of a perfect being. That model is patterned after the behavior of the religious thinkers of mankind who have done more harm than good.

Everything that we are confronting today is a product of the religious thinking of man but that thinking has no answers for the future of mankind. So if you want you have to find answers within the framework of the systems that have failed to deliver the goods. I don't think religious thinking has any answers for our problems today.

* * * * *

Nobody knows anything about life and there is no point in defining it. Anything that we say of life is speculation on our part. What we are trying to understand or experience, life or whatever, is through the help of the knowledge we have of it but thought is something dead. It is something that can never touch anything living. The moment it tries to touch life and capture it, contain it and give expression to it, it is destroyed by the living quality of life. What we mean by life, however, is not actually life but living.

Living is our relationship with the people around us, the life around us, with the whole world around us, and that is all we know. That relationship is actually not a basic relationship but a relationship that is born out of our demand to become one with life. So anything we do, any attempt we make to become one with it, is fruitless because there is no way we can establish any relationship with the life around us.

I am not for a moment assuming or emphasizing that we are not part of it. We are part of it but the most important question which we should ask ourselves is, "What is it that separates us from the life around us and what is it that maintains the separateness or division, if I may use the word, all the time?" Actually, what divides us is thought. Thought is matter but that matter cannot stay there for long.

The moment the matter is born it has to become part of the energy again. But this demand on our part or on the part of thought to maintain continuity is the demand that drives us to experience the same thing over and over and over again. And thus we are maintaining this superficial, artificial, non-existent duality, division there between our life and the life around us.

It is only an assumption on our part, and I would say it is a false assumption, that thoughts are spontaneous and self-generated. They are not. Thought is only a response to stimuli. The brain is not really a creator, it is just a container. The function of the brain in this body is only to take care of the needs of the physical organism and to maintain its sensitivity whereas thought, through its constant interference with sensory activity, is destroying the sensitivity of the body. That is where the conflict is.

The conflict is between the need of the body to maintain its sensitivity and the demand of thought to translate every sensation within the framework of the sensual activity. I am not condemning sensual activity. Mind or whatever you want to call it is born out of this sensuality, so all activities of the mind are sensual in their nature whereas the activity of the body is to respond to the stimuli around it. That is really the basic conflict between what you call the mind and the body. I don't think there is any such thing as mind separate from the activity of the brain.

The body is not interested in sensual activity. It is not interested in any experiences that the mind is interested in and is demanding. It is not even interested in the so-called spiritual experiences, the religious experiences like bliss, beatitude, immensity and happiness. Happiness is something which the body is not interested in. It cannot take it for long. Pleasure is one of the things that it is always rejecting. The body does not know and does not even want to know anything about happiness. Happiness is a cultural input there. Is there any such thing as happiness? I would say, no.

So the quest for happiness is a cultural input and that is the common desire that we know exists everywhere in every part of the world. That is what we all want and that want is the most important want in human beings everywhere. Happiness, if you want to use that word, is like any other sensation. The moment thought separates itself from what is called the sensation of happiness, the demand to keep that sensation going longer than its natural duration also occurs with it.

So any sensation, however extraordinary, however pleasant it may be, is rejected by the body. Keeping that sensation going longer than its duration of life is destroying the sensitivity of the sensory perceptions and sensitivity of this living organism. That is the battle that is going on there. If you do not know what happiness is you will never be unhappy.

* * * * *

There is no individual there at all. Culture, society or whatever you want to call it has created you and me for the sole purpose of maintaining its own continuity but at the same time we are made to believe that you have to become an individual. These two things have created this neurotic situation for us. There is no such thing as an individual and there is no such thing as freedom of action. I am not talking of a fatalistic philosophy or any such thing. It is this fact that is frustrating us.

The demand to fit ourselves into that value system is using a tremendous amount of energy and there is nothing we can do to deal with the living problems here. All the energy is being consumed by the demands of the culture or society or whatever you want to call it to fit you into the framework of that value system. In the process, we are not left with any energy to deal with the other problems. But these problems, that is, the living problems, are very simple. To survive in this world is not a difficult problem, you see. But what is demanding is the value system. Our effort to fit ourselves into that value system is consuming a tremendous amount of energy.

It is just not possible to establish any relationship with anything around you including your near and dear ones except on the level of what you can get out of the relationship. You see, the whole thing springs from this separation or isolation that human beings live in today. We are isolated from the rest of creation, the rest of life around us. We all live in individual frames. We try to establish a relationship at the level of, What do I get out of that relationship? We use others to try and fill this void that is created as a result of our isolation.

We always want to fill this emptiness, this void, with all kinds of relationships with people around us. That is really the problem. We have to use everything "an idea, a person, anything we can get hold of" to establish relationships with others. Without relationships we are lost and we don't see any meaning, we don't see any purpose. This is because your only interest is to create a purposeful and meaningful relationship with the individuals and the world around you. Therefore, you want to understand the reality of the world but there is nothing to understand. There is no such thing as reality at all. Anything you do to understand the reality of the world is not going to be useful,helpful or meaningful.

* * * * *

The living organism is like a computer with an extraordinary intelligence. But here the energy is a sort of expression of life. Energy is already there but you are all the time asking questions. These are two computers talking but you want to introduce an element which is not part of the functioning of this living organism. That is why you begin to think that there must be something different here.

You are more intelligent than I am. You see, this is something which can be measured. We have certain yardsticks in the world that say that you are more intelligent than I am. But any attempt on my part to improve my intelligence, change it, modify it, make it better, would consume tremendous amounts of energy, that is all. You see, without that what you are left with is something extraordinary. It is not interested in comparing itself with your intellect or anything. It is not a question of accepting that I am a low grade moron.

When once it is a fact that there is no movement in any direction of improving, changing or evolving into anything different or better then what is there is something extraordinary. It is unique in its own way. Every individual is unique. Nature creates perfect species, unlike religion and education which attempt to create perfect individuals.

Every human being is different, that is all I am saying. There is nobody like you anywhere in this world. I tell you, nobody! I am talking physiologically, you know. But we ignore that and try to put everybody in a common mold and create what we call the greatest common factor, all the time trying to educate them and fit them into the value system.

If that value system does not work, naturally revolutions take place. The whole idea of restructuring is nothing but a revaluation of the old value system. Revolution only means revaluation of our value system. It is the same thing. After a while things settle down and then they go at it again. There is no improvement again or there is a slight improvement but it is basically a modified continuity of the same. In that process, what horrors we have committed, you know! Is it really worth all that? But you seem to think that it is. After killing so many people you go back to the same system, the same technique. What is the point? But we will keep going that way.

* * * * *

The questions, "Is there any meaning? Is there any purpose?" take away the living quality of life. You are living in a world of ideas. Anything I say would not be of much interest to people. When people ask me whether there is any such thing as reincarnation, my answer is that there is reincarnation for those who believe in it, and there is no reincarnation for those who do not believe in it. It is not a clever answer, because it is the belief which is important.

If you ask a fundamental question, "Is there any such thing as reincarnation as the other laws in nature like gravity?" my answer would be negative, a definite no. It is not as much part of nature as gravity is but if you want to believe that it is so it is a different matter. The belief in reincarnation is born out of the demand that something will continue after your so-called death. It is the same mechanism which wants to know what will happen after death.

For exactly the same reason you are asking the question, "Is there any meaning, is there any purpose in life?" For some reason, that mechanism, that movement of thought, does not want to come to an end. You have seen people dying there. So the belief that there is a center here, that there is a spirit here, that there is a soul here, is what is responsible for that belief that there must be something beyond but if you want to know if there is anything beyond, you have to die now.

When the question or belief about that comes to an end death will take place here right now, clinical death will take place. Then the question whether there is an afterlife would not at all arise because the living organism has no way of knowing that it is alive. The belief has to go. The end of belief is death. But you replace one belief with another, one illusion with another illusion. That is all that we are doing.

* * * * *

Wherever there is division there can't be love. We are trying to bridge this gap, which is horrible for us, which has no meaning, which is demanding something from us, with this fancy idea that there must be love between these two individuals. Obviously, our relationships are not so loving. So we want to somehow make them into loving affairs, loving relationships.

What an amount of energy we are putting into making our relationship into a loving thing! It is a battle, a war. It is like preparing yourself all the time for war hoping that there will be peace, eternal peace, or this or that. You are tired of this battle and you even settle for that horrible, non-loving relationship. And you hope and dream one day it will be nothing but love. "Love thy neighbor as thyself. In the name of that, how many millions of people have been killed? More than all the recent wars put together. How can you love thy neighbor as thyself? It is just not possible. Obviously, otherwise why are so many people, women, children and helpless people killed?

* * * * *

Sexuality, if it is left to itself as it is in the case of other species, other forms of life, is merely a biological need because the living organism has this object to survive and produce one like itself. Anything you superimpose on that is totally unrelated to the living organism. But we have turned that, what you call sexual activity, which is biological in its nature, into a pleasure movement. I am not saying anything against the pleasure movement. I am not interested in saying that you should condemn that or become promiscuous or use sex as a means of spiritual attainment; no. It is a very simple functioning of the living organism. The religious man has turned that into something big and concentrated on the control of sex. After that the psychologists have turned that into something extraordinary.

All commercialism is related to sex. How do you think it will fall into its proper place? I am just pointing out the use to which we are putting that simple biological function. I am not condemning it. It is there, you see. Your talk of that as an expression of love has no meaning to me. We would love to put it that way because it is very comforting. If sex is used only for the biological purpose it is not really a devastating situation. If you leave it as it is it wouldn't be so horrible, the way you would like to put it, it would fall into its proper place. That is why we have invented all these other things "God, truth, and reality" which are nothing but ultimate pleasures.

* * * * *

Look at this moment. It's wonderful! I don't write poetry. The next moment I am looking at you, you are as beautiful as the ocean there, probably more beautiful. You see, if I am freed from all the ideas that I have of beauty, there is something that is extraordinary there. Nothing needs to be done to change anything. Things are changing in their own ways.

* * * * *

We are afraid of coming to an end. There is nothing here to come to an end. Nothing will come to an end except the one that does not want to come to an end. It is interested in preserving itself somehow, in some way, even beyond death. You see, it is not going to succeed.

5. 1990: Various Places

There is no process to go through to reach anywhere. It looks like I went through some process. No, I did not. I wasted so many years of my life in pursuit of the goals that I had set for myself. If it had dawned on me during the early stages of my life that there is nothing to understand, I wouldn't have wasted all that time. But I don't see any way of comparing what I did with what I stumbled into.

The fundamental mistake that humanity made somewhere along the line was to experience this separateness from the totality of life. At that time, there occurred in people this self-consciousness which separated them from the life around. They were so isolated that it frightened them. The demand to be part of the totality of life created this tremendous demand for the ultimate. We thought that the spiritual goals of God, truth or reality would help us to become part of the whole again but the very attempt to become one or integrated with the totality of life has kept us only more separate.

Isolated functioning is not part of nature. This isolation has created a demand for finding out ways and means of becoming a part of nature. But thought, in its very nature, can only create problems and cannot help us solve them. We don't seem to realize that it is thought that is separating us from the totality of things. The belief that this can help us to keep in tune with the totality is not going to materialize. So it has come up with all kinds of ingenious, if I may use that word, ideas of insight and intuition.

What we are concerned about is living, our relationship with our fellow beings, with the life around. By understanding the meaning of life and the purpose of life we are not going to improve, change, modify or alter our behavior patterns in any way. But there is a hope that by understanding the meaning of life we can bring about a change. There may not be any meaning of life. If it has a meaning it is already in operation there. Wanting to understand the meaning of life seems to be a futile attempt on our part.

We have been for centuries told what to do. Why are we asking the same question, What to do? What to do in relation to what? What I am emphasizing is that the demand to bring about a change in ourselves is the cause of our suffering.

I may say that there is nothing to be changed but the revolutionary teachers come and tell us that there is something there in which you have to bring about a radical revolution then we assume there is such a thing as soul, spirit or the self. What I assert all the time is that I haven't found anything like the self or soul there.

This question haunted me all my life and suddenly it hit me, There is no self to realize. What the hell have I been doing all this time? You see, that hits you like lightning. Once that hits you, the whole mechanism of the body that is controlled by this thought is shattered. What is left is the tremendous living organism with an intelligence of its own. What you are left with is the pulse, the beat and the throb of life.

There must be something more and we have to do something to become part of the whole thing. Such demands have arisen because of our assumption that we have been created for a grander purpose than that for which other species on this planet have been created. That's the fundamental mistake we have made. Culture is responsible for our assuming this. We thus come to believe that the whole creation is for the benefit of man. The demand to use nature for our purposes has created all the ecological problems. It is not such an easy thing for us to deal with these problems.

The point is we have probably arrived at a place where there is no going back. What is the fate of mankind and what is one to do? Anything that is born out of thought is destructive in its nature. That is why I very often say in my conversations and interviews that thought in its birth, in its nature, in its expression and in its action is fascist.

* * * * *

I do not see any meaning or purpose in life. A living thing, a living organism, is not interested in such questions. Don't superimpose varieties of religious experience on nature. Your doing something to go back to your natural state is what is taking you away from it. The natural state is already there and is expressing itself in an extraordinarily intelligent way. The acquired intellect is no match to the intelligence that is there.

* * * * *

I was surrounded by all kinds of religious people. I felt that there was something funny in their behavior. There was a wide gap between what they believed and how they lived. This always bothered me but I could not call all of them hypocrites. I said to myself, There is something wrong with what they believe. Maybe their source is wrong. All the teachers of mankind, particularly the spiritual teachers, conned themselves and conned the whole of mankind. So I have to find out for myself and I have no way of finding out anything for myself as long as I depend upon anyone.

I found that whatever I wanted was what they wanted me to want. Whatever I thought was whatever they wanted me to think. So there was no way out of this. Somewhere along the line something hit me, There is nothing there to be transformed, nothing there to be changed. There is no mind there nor is there any self to realize. What the hell am I doing?

That spark hit me like a shaft of lightning, like an earthquake. It shattered the whole structure of my thought and destroyed everything that was there, all the cultural input. It hit me in a very strange way. Everything that every man had ever thought, felt and experienced before was drained out of my system. In a way, it totally destroyed my mind which is nothing but the totality of man's experiences and thoughts. It destroyed even my identity.

* * * * *

You want to become something other than what you are. That creates this neurotic situation. The neurosis in the human species is absolutely essential. We have to maintain this neurosis in order to function in this society. There is no other way that we can function in this society except to live in hope and die in hope. There are some people who have given up but we force them to become functional in this value system which we have created. We even push them to commit suicide lest they become manic-depressive individuals. We are solely responsible for driving all these people into a situation where they have to put an end to themselves. They don't want to be functional here, they have given up. That is the reason why I say that the psychiatrist is the enemy of this culture because he is forcing all those people who have given up to fit into this value system.

Nature is trying to create something extraordinary, a perfect species. That is why each individual is unique. Because of this input of culture it has become impossible for this organism to show uniqueness. We have destroyed the possibility of what nature can do. You only use this paradise that nature has created including not only mankind but all the species that exist on this planet. We are solely and fully responsible for the chaos that mankind has created and there seems to be no way out of it.

Every time a so-called savior comes along he says that he is an avatar and that he is the answer to all our problems. This very thing, his claim that he is the answer, adds momentum to the existing chaos and that situation makes it impossible for us to create something new. That is not the way we can resolve our problems.

If they are looking for answers they should not look to Vedanta or Zen Buddhism. Those sects don't have any answers for their problems. The scientists and psychologists have to find their answers, if there are any answers, within their own framework. Only then will they be able to help mankind to look at things differently. But there is no way you can go back and revive anything.

* * * * *

Once a holy man came to see me. He was claiming that denial of sex is so essential for the spiritual future of man. I said, It's a crime against nature. Nature has not intended you to deny sex. Then he got up and left. How can that abnormal situation be made a model for all spiritual aspirants and why torture them? Why has denial of sex been made the foundation of spiritual enlightenment? As a reaction or a revolt against that, what you call the tantric system appeared in this country.

To be attracted is natural. If you are not attracted you are a stone. The body, with its senses, is not a stone. It has to respond to what is happening around it. What touches this body is not your piety or your silence but your anger, your lust and everything that is happening there. That is the response I am talking about.

The actions of life are outside the field of thought. Life is simply a process of stimulus and response, and stimulus and response are one unitary movement. But it is thought that separates them and says that this is the response and that is the stimulus. Any action that is born out of thinking is destructive in its nature because thought is a self-perpetuating mechanism. Any action that is outside the field of thought is one continuous movement, it is one with the movement of life. It is that flow of things that I am referring to, you see.

To sidestep the complexities of life is one of the biggest mistakes that we are making. But there is nothing out there, you see. All these godmen, gurus and the flunkies (the most wicked word to use) are offering us a new oasis. You will find out that it is no different from other mirages. We are leaving everything for some mythical certainty offered to us. But this is the only reality, there is no other reality.

What I am emphasizing is if your energy is not wasted in pursuit of some mythical certainties offered to us, life becomes very simple. But we end up being wasted, misled and misspent individuals. If that energy is released, what is it that we can't do to survive in the midst of these complexities of the world created by our culture? It is very simple. The attempt to sidestep these complexities is the very thing that is causing us all these problems.

What I am saying is not what the mainstream of population is interested in. They hear what they want to hear. What I say is of no interest to them. If you say that God is redundant it is not a rebellion against anything. You know religious thinking is outdated and outmoded. But I go one step further and say that all political ideologies are nothing but the outgrowth of the same religious thinking of man. What I am suggesting is that the very demand to understand the mystery of existence is destructive. Just leave the mystery alone.

* * * * *

There was this makeup within me, from the very beginning, of rejecting everything totally. I lived amongst masterminds. They were not ordinary people. I have traveled everywhere and, as I say, I was not born yesterday. I did not come into town in a turnip truck. What I am saying is that this is something that you cannot totally reject through any volition or effort of yours. Somehow it happened to me. It is just a happening. The whole thing drained out of my system. The parameters that mankind has evolved, the thoughts, feelings and experiences throughout the ages, all this was thrown out of my system.

It's a miracle. What I am emphasizing is that whatever has happened to me has happened despite everything I did. In fact, everything I did only blocked it. It prevented the possibility of whatever was there to express itself. Not that I have gained anything, only that what is there is able to express itself without any hindrance, without any constraints or restraints imposed on it by society for its own reasons, for its own continuity and stability.

The search is inevitable and is an integral part of it. That is why it has turned us all into neurotics and has created this duality for us. You see, ambition is a reality, competition is a reality, but you have superimposed on that reality the idea that you should not be ambitious. It has turned us all into neurotic individuals. We want two things at the same time. The demands for pleasure and happiness have created the whole religious thinking God, truth or reality.

We demand that there must be something permanent. That is what these religious teachers are peddling. They claim to offer you eternal happiness. Are they ready to accept the fact that bliss, love and compassion are also sensual? This certainty that I have is something that I cannot transmit to you. It does not mean that I will go and burn all the churches and temples or bury all the scriptures (that's all too silly) or that I will become a terrorist and mindlessly kill everyone.

* * * * *

You are only trying to fit me into a framework by calling me an enlightened man but you have not arrived anywhere. Even the claimants have not arrived anywhere. There is no other way I can point out the danger that is involved in your seeking whatever you are seeking. You see, there is this pleasure movement. I am not against the pleasure movement. I am neither preaching hedonism nor advocating any ism or anything. What I am saying is a threat to you as you know yourself and experience yourself so you necessarily have to fit me into that framework. Or else, you put it another way and say that the content of whatever has happened to U.G. and to them is the same but his expression is different.

The natural state is the functioning of this living organism. It is not a synonymous term for enlightenment or God-realization or self-realization. What is left here is this pulsating, living organism. It is outside the field of experience, so it cannot be shared with anyone. That's the reason why I am saying that he, you or it is the medium through which whatever I am saying is expressing itself but you are distorting, correlating and garbling it. Thought cannot help doing that.

From then on, understanding is not through the instrument which we are using all the time to understand, the intellect. We have developed and sharpened the intellect through years. So it understood in its own way that it is not the instrument, that there is no other instrument and that there is nothing to understand.

My problem was how to use this intellect to understand whatever I was looking for but it didn't help me to understand a thing. So I was searching for some other instrument to understand, that is, intuition, this, that and the other. But I realized that this is the only instrument I have and the hope that I would understand something through some other instrument, on some other level and some other way, disappeared. It dawned on me, There is nothing to understand. When this happened it hit me like a shaft of lightning.

From then on, the very demand to understand anything was finished. That understanding is the one that is expressing itself now and it cannot be used as an instrument to understand anything. It cannot be used as an instrument to guide, direct or help me, you or anybody. That explosion that occurred is happening all the time. It is all the time exploding.

Any attempt on my part to understand anything at any given moment is exploded because that is the only instrument I have and there is no other instrument. This instrument cannot invent a thing called hope anymore. There is no hope of understanding. The moment it is forming something there it is exploded, not through any volition, not through any effort, but that's exactly the way it happens. It is continuously happening all the time.

That is the way life is moving along. It has no direction. The body has no need to understand anything. The body does not have to learn anything because anything you learn, anything you do, is attempting to change, alter, shape or mold yourself into something better. This is a perfect piece that has been created by nature.

* * * * *

There is nothing to die here. The body cannot be afraid of death. The movement that is created by society or culture is what does not want to come to an end. How it came to an end I really don't know. What you are afraid of is not death. In fact, you don't want to be free from fear because when the fear comes to an end you will drop dead. That is its nature. It is the fear that makes you believe that you are living and that you will be dead. What you call yourself is fear. The you is born out of fear, lives in fear, functions in fear and dies in fear.

When the body encounters a cobra it steps back and then you take a walk. The cobra is a marvelous creature. If you hurt it you are hurting yourself. I mean it physically hurts you, not psychologically or romantically, because it is all one movement of life. What I am saying is that you will never hurt that. The cooperation there springs from the total selfishness of mutual survival. It is that total interdependence for survival on the physical level that can bring about unity.

The intelligence that is necessary for survival is already there in the physical organism, you don't have to learn a thing. You need to be taught, you need to learn things, only to survive in this world which we have created, the world of ideas. You have to fight for your piece of the pie. Some joker comes along and says that you should fight without expecting any results. What the hell are you talking about? How can you act without expecting any results?

As long as you live in this world you have to fight for your fair share. That is why they teach you, send you to a school and give you some tools. That is what society has done to you but religion comes along and tells you that you should fight for your share without expecting anything in return. That is why you are turned into a neurotic individual. Otherwise, you will fight only for your share. You don't grab the whole thing. You grab the whole thing because you have been taught by religion, culture or something else to do so. Animals kill only for their survival and leave the rest of their game. Every other thing survives on that. When one takes only what is really needed, the rest is there for everyone else, there's plenty.

* * * * *

Man has created religion because it gives him a cover. You see, good and bad, right and wrong are like the two ends of the spectrum, one cannot exist independent of the other. When once you are finished with this duality (I am using the word with much caution although I don't like to use it), when you are no longer caught up in the dichotomy of right and wrong or good and bad, you can never do anything wrong. As long as you are caught up in it the danger is that you will always do wrong and if you don't do wrong it is because you are a frightened chicken. It is out of this cowardice that the whole religious thinking is born.

* * * * *

Nothing has happened to me. You and I are functioning in exactly the same way and I am not anything that you are not. You think that I am different from you. I know for certain that you are functioning in exactly the same way that I am functioning but you are trying to channel the activity or movement of life both to get something and to maintain that continuity of what is put in there by culture. That is not the case here.

* * * * *

What has created the space between creation and destruction or the time between the two is thought. In nature, there is no death or destruction at all. What occurs is the reshuffling of atoms. If there is a need or necessity to maintain the balance of energy in this universe, death occurs. You may not like it. Earthquakes may be condemned by us. Surely they cause misery to so many thousands and thousands of people. And all this humanitarian activity around the world to send supplies is really a commendable act. It helps those who are suffering. But it is the same kind of activity that is responsible for killing millions of people. What I am saying is that war and humanitarianism are born from the same source.

* * * * *

The self-consciousness that occurred in the human species may be a necessary thing, I don't know. I am not claiming that I have a special insight into the workings of nature. You see for yourself. That's why I say that the very foundation of the human culture is to kill and to be killed. It has happened so. If one is interested in looking at history right from the beginning, the whole foundation of humanity is built on the idea that those who are not with us are against us. That's what is operating in human thinking. So to kill and to be killed in the name of God, represented by the church in the West and all the other religious thinking here in the East, was the order of the day. That's why there is fundamentalism.

* * * * *

The body is not interested in your techniques of meditation which actually are destroying the peace that is already there. It is an extraordinarily peaceful organism. It does not have to do anything to be in a peaceful state. By introducing this idea of a peaceful mind we set in motion a sort of battle that goes on and on. What you regard as peaceful is in actuality nothing more than a war-weary state of mind.

* * * * *

Every insight you have is born out of your thinking. Your so-called insights merely strengthen and fortify the very thing you are trying to be free from. All insights, however extraordinary they may be, are worthless. You can create a tremendous structure of thought from your own discovery which you call insight but that insight is nothing but the result of your own thinking, the permutations and combinations of thought. Actually, there is no way you can come up with anything original there.

There is no thought which you can call your own. I don't have any thoughts which I can call my own not one thought, not one word, not one experience. To experience anything you have to depend upon outside knowledge.

The recognition of yourself as an entity is possible only through the help of the knowledge. We start this process with children. We do not want that identity to come to an end. We do everything possible to maintain it but the effort to maintain your identity is wearing you out. The constant use of memory to maintain our identity eventually puts us in a state where we are forced to give up yet when someone gives up the attempt to fit themself into the value system they are scorned.

Even when we discover the laws of nature, for whatever reason we are interested in doing so, ultimately they are used to destroy everything that nature has created. This propaganda that the planet is in danger is media hype. Everybody has in fact forgotten about it. We are not ready to face this situation squarely. We must not look for answers in the past or in the great heritage of this or that nation and we must not look to the religious thinkers. They don't have any answers.

I am not prophesying that there is going to be a paradise on earth, nothing of the sort. There is not going to be any paradise. It is the idea of a paradise, the idea of creating a heaven on earth that has turned this beautiful paradise that we already have on this planet into a hell. We are solely responsible for what is happening and the answers for our problems cannot come from the past and its glory or from the great religious teachers of mankind. Those teachers will naturally claim that you all have failed and that they have the answers for the problems that we are confronted with today. I don't think that they have any answers. We have to find out the answers if there are any for ourselves and by ourselves.

It is amazing that we have tremendous faith in all these religious people who cannot deliver the goods. In a business deal, if your partner refuses or fails to deliver the goods, that is the end of the business relationship but in the area of religion they can get away with just promising something. They don't deliver the goods at all. How we can fall for that kind of a thing is beyond me. The whole con game has gone on for centuries. Why do we allow ourselves to be conned by those con men?

There is not a single exception all these spiritual teachers of mankind from the very beginning have conned themselves into the belief that they have the answers, the solutions for mankind. They cannot deliver the goods. They only give us hope.

When once the demand to change yourself into something better, something other than what you actually are ceases, the demand to change the world also comes to an end. The world can't be anything different from what we are. If there is a war going on within us we cannot expect a peaceful world around us, we will certainly create war.

This instrument is only interested in perpetuating itself through what it calls understanding which in reality is its own machinations. Nature creates something then it destroys it and creates something else. The comparative process characteristic of thinking seems to be absent. The whole ethical culture that is built by us to shape the actions of man has totally failed.

I don't want many people. I am trying to avoid all the seekers and if there are any finders they don't need my help. By allowing myself to be surrounded by those people I am inadvertently participating in the illusion that by carrying on a dialogue or a conversation with me they are getting something. So I discourage people. Even if they just come and sit around me I try to point out the ridiculous nature of this get together. I try to finish it by saying, Nice meeting you all, but still they don't go. They would sit with me for hours and hours. Even if I get up and go away they would be still there sitting and talking. They would be talking about what I did or did not say or what they thought I had said.

Still they keep coming back. Most of those who come to see me are religious buffs of all shapes, sizes and colors. Unless they have some sort of background in all this they can't be interested in this kind of thing. They only come to receive some confirmation from me about what they are interested in but they find that they are not getting anything from me. Still they continue to come. You have no idea of how many thousands of people have passed through the precincts of my homes.

Some of them are intelligent enough to realize that they are not going to get anything from me and that there is no point in hanging around. Others are not ready to accept what I emphasize, overemphasize and assert all the time, that whatever has happened to me has happened despite everything I did. Some friends who have been with me for years say that they still have the hope that they are going to get something from me. This, in short, is the story of my life. If you destroy the authority of others, you in your own way become an authority.

The whole structure of religious thought is built on the foundation of discipline. Discipline to me means a sort of masochism. We are all masochists. We torture ourselves because we think that suffering is a means to achieve our spiritual goals. That's unfortunate. Life is difficult so discipline sounds very attractive to people. We admire those who have suffered a lot to achieve their goals. As a matter of fact, the whole religious thinking is built on the foundation of suffering. Those who impose that kind of discipline on us are sadists and we are all being masochists in accepting that. We torture ourselves in the hope of achieving something.

We are slaves to our ideas and beliefs. We are not ready to throw them out. If we succeed in throwing them out we replace them with another set of beliefs, another body of discipline. Those who are marching into the battlefield and are ready to be killed today in the name of democracy, in the name of freedom, in the name of communism are no different from those who threw themselves to the lions in the arenas. The Romans watched that fun with great joy. How are we different from them? Not a bit. We love it. To kill and to be killed is the foundation of our culture.

* * * * *

We are not honest, decorous and decent enough to admit that all relationships are built on the foundation of, What do I get out of this relationship It is nothing but mutual gratification. If that is absent no relationship is possible. You keep the relationship going for social reasons or for reasons of children, property and security. All this is part and parcel of the relationship business but when it fails and does not give us what we really want we superimpose on it what we call love. So it is just not possible to have any relationship on any basis except on the level of mutual gratification.

The whole culture has created this situation for us through its value system. The value system demands that relationships be based on love, but the most important elements are security and possessiveness. When your hold on the other weakens, the relationship wears out. You cannot maintain this lovey-dovey relationship all the time.

The relationship between a man and a woman is based on the images that the two create for themselves of each other. So the actual relationship between the two individuals is a relationship between the two images. But your image keeps changing and so does the other person's. To keep the image constant is just not possible. So when everything else fails we use this final, last card in the pack, love, with all the marvelous and romantic ideations around it.

To me, love implies two. Wherever there is a division, whether it is within you or without you, there is conflict. That relationship cannot last long. As far as I am concerned, relationships are formed and then they are dissolved immediately. Both these things happen in the same frame, if I may use that word. That is really the problem. You may think that I am a very crude man but if anybody talks to me about love, to me it is a four letter word. That is the only basic relationship between man and woman, but it is a social problem for us as to what kind of a relationship you should have.

Unfortunately, we have blown this business of sex out of proportion. It is just a simple biological need of the living organism. But sex has become a tremendous problem for us because we have turned the basic biological functioning of the body into a pleasure movement. You see, if there is no thought, there is no sex at all. It is not just the sex act that is important but the build-up that is there, the romantic structure that we have built around the love play.

Here, the build-up is totally absent because there is no way to focus on any particular object continuously. So you see, that has moved from there to here and again from here to something else, as perhaps, to her movements. It is constantly changing its focus and there is no way that you can maintain this build-up. What is there is only the physical attraction. That you can never be free from, ever. All those people, these saints, are tortured with the idea of controlling that natural attraction, but that natural attraction is something which should not be condemned.

You don't tell yourself that you are a god man, realized or enlightened, and that you should not think these thoughts. Why the religious thinking of man has emphasized denial of sex as a means to his spiritual attainment is something that I cannot understand. Maybe because that is the way you can control people.

Sex is the most powerful drive. After all, the sex glands have to function. We cannot accept the fact that we are just biological beings and nothing more. It is something like saying that in the field of economics you are not controlled by the laws of supply and demand. But we are not ready to accept the basic, fundamental fact that we are just biological beings and all that is happening within the body is a result of hormonal activity. It is pure and simple chemistry. Problems in that area cannot be solved in any other way than by trying to change the chemistry of the body. I think our whole thinking has to be put on a different track. It is all chemical. If, as they say, desires are hormones, then the whole ethical code and culture that we have created through centuries to control the behavior of human beings are false.

So desire cannot be false. Anything that is happening within the organism cannot be false. There is no sex at all without thought. Thought is memory. These experts make fun of me when I say that one of the most important of all glands is the thymus gland. When I discussed this subject with some physiologists and doctors they made fun of me. Naturally so, because according to them the gland is inactive. If it is activated through any external means it would be an abnormal situation. But the thymus is one of the most important glands and feelings operate there without the element of thought.

You see, medical technology has ignored that for a very long time. They considered any unusual condition of the gland to be an abnormality and tried to treat it. It is true that when you reach adolescence it becomes inactive and then your feelings are controlled by your ideas. When once this kind of disturbance takes place in the hormonal balance of the human body through this catastrophe, through this calamity, through whatever you want to call it, not only is the thymus activated but also all other glands such as the pineal and the pituitary are activated.

What I have against medical technology is that you want to understand the functioning of these things with a motive. When once you have some idea of how these glands function, how the activation of these things will help mankind, you are not going to use it for the benefit of mankind. What I am trying to say is that the feelings felt at the thymus are quite different from the feelings induced by thoughts.

Sex has to be put in its proper place as one of the natural functionings of the body. It is solely, mainly and wholly for the purpose of reproducing or procreating something like this. It has no other place in the functioning of the body. Thought always interferes with sex. It has become a pleasure movement. I am not saying anything against it. After that it goes. Thereafter, what you are left with is the natural functioning of the glands.

So we have to revise all our ideas about this whole business of sex. We give a tremendous importance to sex and so the denial of it becomes such an obsession with people. In India, they even moved away from that denial and created what is called tantric sex. It was the highest pleasure that human beings could have, sex through tantra was considered the highest.

The fact is that the person is very much there even at the moment when there is peak sex experience. The experience has already been captured by your memory. Otherwise, you have no way of experiencing that as a peak moment. If that peak moment remained as a peak moment that would be just the end of sex. That would be the end of everything. The fact that you remember it as a peak moment and want to repeat it over and over again implies that it has already become part of your experiencing structure. You want it always and then want to extend it for longer and longer periods of time.

All these things I observed myself. I did not learn about them from anyone. I saw them happen in my own life. I denied myself sex for twenty-five years pursuing spiritual goals. Then I suddenly realized, Look, this is ridiculous. Celibacy has nothing to do with it. Sex is burning inside of me. Why the hell am I denying myself sex? Why the hell am I torturing myself That did not mean that I moved to the other extreme and practiced promiscuity as my way of life. Sex is violence but it is a necessary pain for this body.

All creative things are painful. The birth of a child is a very natural thing but to call it a traumatic experience and build up a tremendous structure of theories around it is something I am not concerned with. It cannot be a traumatic experience. To continue with what I was saying, that is why after all this violence you go to sleep. You feel tired. That is how nature functions. All creations in nature are like that. Volcanic eruptions, earthquakes, storms and floods are all part of nature. You cannot say that there is only chaos or that there is only order. Chaos and order, like birth and death, are simultaneous processes.

What I want to say is that, unfortunately, society, culture or whatever you want to call it has separated the sex activity and put it on a different level instead of treating it as a simple functioning of the living organism. It is a basic thing in nature. Survival and reproduction are basic things in the living organisms.

Look, anything we touch we turn into a problem and sex even more so because this is the most powerful drive there is. If you translate it and push it into an area where it does not really belong, namely the pleasure movement, we will then create problems. When once you create a problem, the demand to deal with that problem within that framework is bound to arise. That problem has to be solved by people, otherwise they become neurotic. They don't know what to do with themselves. Not only that but everything God, truth, reality, liberation is ultimate pleasure. We are not ready to accept that.

Sex has become a very powerful factor in our lives. That is why there is also a demand to put limitations on it by culture, first in the name of religion and then in the name of the family, law, war and a hundred other things. You talk of the sacredness of life and condemn abortion and then you go and kill millions of people in the name of your flag, in the name of patriotism. That is the way things are. You first create a tension. All this fantasy, all this romantic nonsense, is building up tension.

* * * * *

It's really unfortunate that man got away with everything for centuries while society ignored women. Half the population of this planet was neglected, humiliated and treated as doormats. Even the Bible story tells you that the woman is made out of the rib of man. What preposterous nonsense! The other party is also responsible for that. You are praising the woman as a darling and she accepts that minor role. The woman is also to be blamed for it. I am not overly enthusiastic about all these feminist movements today. It is a revolt that really has no basis. It's more of a reaction.

One of the leaders of the feminist movement visited me and asked, What do you have to say of our movement I said, I am on your side but you have to realize one very fundamental thing. As long as you depend on man for your sexual needs, so long you are not a free person. If you use a vibrator for your sexual satisfaction, that is a different matter. You are very crude, she said. I am not crude. What I am saying is a fact. As long as you depend upon something or somebody there is scope for exploitation.

There was a time when I believed that if women were to rule this world it would be a different story. We had a woman prime minister in India and a woman prime minister in Sri Lanka. There was a lady prime minister in England. But I tell you they are as ruthless as any others; in fact, more ruthless. This dream of mine was shattered when I saw that woman there in Jerusalem. So it is not a question of a man running the show or a woman running the show. It is the system that corrupts.

Now they are talking of hormones. They say that it is the hormones that are responsible for the violence. If that is so what do we do? Assuming for a moment that the advantage that we have had for centuries is not a culturally instigated thing but a hormonal phenomenon, you have to deal with it in a different way and not put that person on the couch, analyze him and say that his mother or his great-grandmother was responsible for his aggression. That is too absurd and silly. So we have to find some way.

The basic question which we have to ask for ourselves is, What kind of a human being do you want Unfortunately, we have placed before ourselves the model of a perfect being. The perfect being is a god man or a spiritual man or an avatar or some such being. But forcing everyone to fit into that mold is the cause of our tragedy. It is just not possible for us all to be like that.

Once upon a time, the scepter and the crown, the church and the pontiffs, were all worshiped. Later, the kings revolted against that and then the royal family came to be admired and worshiped. Where are they now? Others have eliminated royalty and have created the office of the president. We are told that you should not insult the head of the state. Until yesterday he was your neighbor and now he becomes the president of your republic. Why do you have to worship a king or a president? The whole hierarchical structure, whether of the past or of the present, is exactly the same.

This has no value in the sense that whatever I am cannot be fitted into any value system. It is of no use for the world. It has no value for me and it has no value for the world. You may very well ask me the question, Why the hell are we talking about all this? Because you had some questions to throw at me and what I am doing is to put them in a proper perspective. I only say, Look at it this way.

I am not interested in winning you over to my point of view because I have no point of view and there is no way you can win me over to your point of view. It is not that I am dogmatic or any such thing. During a conversation like this somebody throws at me words like, Oh, you are very this and very that. Alright, I say, This is my point of view. What the hell is yours? It is also a point of view.

So how do you think these two points of view can be reconciled and for what purpose do you want to reconcile them? You feel good because you have won someone to your point of view. You use your logic and your rationality because you are more intelligent than I am. All this is nothing but a power play. You feel good like the people who claim to render service to mankind. That is the do-gooder's high. It is a self-centered activity. You shamelessly tell others that you are doing a social turn. It is just like any other high. If I admit this, living becomes very simple. You are doing it for yourself and you tell others and yourself that you are doing it for the benefit of others.

I believe that the problems of this planet can be solved through the help of the tremendous technology at our disposal. But the benefits that we have accrued through these advancements have not yet percolated to the level of all the people living on this planet. Technology has benefited only a microscopic number of people. When nature has provided us with such bounty, why is it that people are underfed? Why are they starving?

How do we change a human being and for what purpose? If any changes are necessary in human beings and if you want them to function differently by freeing them from all the things that the ethical, cultural, legal structure is failing to free them from and thereby create a different kind of people then probably only genetic engineering could come to our aid. Codes of ethics, morals and the legal structure are not going to help. They have not helped so far. They have not achieved anything.

Our pushing people into a value system is a very undesirable thing, you know. You want to push everybody into a value system. We never question that this value system which we have cherished for centuries may be the very thing that is responsible for our misery. But through the help of genetic engineering we may be able to free individuals from thieving tendencies, from violence, greed and jealousy.

If you are lucky enough to find yourself where there is no attempt on your part to get out of the trap then it may be a different story. But the fact of the matter is that the more you try to get out of the trap the more deeply you are entrenched in it. This is very difficult to understand. I tell all those who want to discuss with me the question of how to decondition yourself, how to live with an unconditioned mind, that the very thing that they are doing is conditioning them, conditioning them in a different way. You are just picking up a new lingo instead of using the usual one. You begin to use the new lingo and feel good, that's all. But this is conditioning you in exactly the same way. That's all it can do. The physical body is conditioned in such a way that it acts as intelligence. Conditioning is intelligence here. There is no need for you to think.

The conditioning of the body is its intelligence. That is the native intelligence of the body. I am not talking about instinct. The intelligence of the body is necessary for its survival. That intelligence is quite different from the intellect which we have developed. Our intellect is no match for that intelligence. If you don't think, the body can take care of itself in a situation where it finds itself in danger. Whenever the body is faced with danger it relies upon itself and not your thinking or your intellect. If, on the other hand, you just think then you are frightened. The fear makes it difficult for you to act.

People ask me, How come you take walks with the cobras? I have never done it with a tiger or any other wild animal but I don't think I would be frightened of them either. If there is no fear in you then you can take walks with them. Fear emits certain odors which the cobra senses. The cobra senses that you are a dangerous thing. Naturally, the cobra has to take the first step. It is one of the most beautiful creatures that nature has created. They are the most lovable creatures. You can take a walk with them and you can talk to them.

I don't know, once a friend of mine, a movie star, visited me in an ashram that I was staying in. She asked me whether it was all an exaggeration that cobras visited me and that I took walks with them. I said, You wait till the evening or night and you will be surprised. Later when we went for a walk at dusk not just one cobra but its wife, children and grandchildren, about fifteen of them, appeared out of nowhere. My guest ran away. If you try to play with it you are in trouble. It is your fear that is responsible for the situation you find yourself in. It is your fear that creates a problem for the cobra. Then it has to take the first step.

If the cobra kills you, you are only one person whereas we kill hundreds and thousands of cobras for no reason. If you destroy these cobras then the field mice will have a field day and you will find that they destroy the crops. If I find a cobra trying to harm a child or somebody I would tell him or tell the cobra to go away. You know, the cobra will go away. But you on the other hand have to kill. Why do you have to kill for no reason? The fear that they will harm us in the future is what is responsible for such acts but we are creating an imbalance in nature.

Because of the constant use of memory, which is thought, to maintain identity, many of the glands which are very essential for the functioning of the living organism have remained dormant, inert and inactive. The pineal gland is, like the thymus, one of the most important glands. That is why they called it the ajÃ±a chakra. If it is activated in a natural way it will take over and give directions to the functioning of this body without thought interfering all the time.

When I use the term natural state it is not a synonym for enlightenment, freedom or God-realization and so forth, not at all. When the totality of mankind's knowledge and experience loses its stranglehold on the body, the physical organism, then the body is allowed to function in its own harmonious way. Your natural state is a biological, neurological and physical state.

We function in a thought sphere and not in our biology. The separative thought structure which is the totality of man's thoughts, feelings, experiences and so onâwhat we call psyche or soul or self"is creating the disturbance. That is what is responsible for our misery. That's what continues the battle that is going on there all the time. This interloper, the thought sphere, has created your entire value system.

The body is not in the least interested in values, much less a value system. It is only concerned with intelligent, moment to moment survival and nothing else. Spiritual values have no meaning to it. When through some miracle or chance you are freed from the hold of thought and culture you are left with the body's natural functions and nothing else. It then functions without the interference of thought.

Nature does not use models. No two leaves are the same. No two faces are the same. No two human beings are the same. I say that no change is necessary, period. Your corrupt society has put into you this notion of change, that you are this and you must be that. Anything that insists that you be something other than what you in fact are is the very thing that is falsifying you and the world.

I somehow stumbled into this natural state on my own and I cannot under any circumstances transmit it to others. It has no social, political, commercial or transformational value to anyone. I do not sit upon platforms haranguing you, demanding that you change the world. As things are, you and the world, which are not two separate things, cannot be any different.

All these attempts on the part of man to change himself go entirely against the way nature is operating. That is why I am not interested. Sorry! Take it or leave it, it's up to you. Whether you praise me or insult me I am not in the least interested. It is your affair. I don't fit into the picture at all. I am only talking about it in response to your questions. You throw the ball and it bounces back. There is no urge in me to express myself to you or anyone else.

You want to make something of what I am saying, to use it somehow to further your own aims. You may say that it is for humanity's sake but really you don't give a damn about society at all. What I am saying cannot possibly be of any use to you or your society. It can only put an end to you as you know yourself. Neither is what I am saying of any use to me because I cannot set up any holy business and make money, it is just impossible for me. I have no interest in freeing you at all. I don't believe in altering you in any way or saving or reforming society or doing anything for mankind.

Society cannot be interested in what I am talking about. Because I am a direct threat to you individually as you know and experience yourself, I am also a threat to society. How can society possibly be interested in this sort of thing? Not a chance. Society is the sum of relationships and, despite what you may find agreeable to believe, all these relationships are sordid and horrible. This is the unsavory fact, take it or leave it. You cannot help but superimpose over these ugly relationships a soothing, fictitious veneer of loving, compassionate and harmonious relationships.

All you know is separateness and duration, space and time, which is the frame superimposed by the mind over the flow of life. But anything that happens in space and time is limiting the energy of life. What life is I don't know nor will I ever. You can say that life is this, that or the other and give hundreds of definitions but the definitions do not capture life. It's like a flowing river. It is only your fear of something coming to an end that is the problem. The ending of fear is the ending of you as you know yourself.

To me the question of whether God exists or not is irrelevant and immaterial. We have no use for God. We have used God to justify the killing of millions and millions of people. We exploit God. You don't want to read your own history. It's full of violence from the beginning to the end.